THE BHAGAVAD-GITA IN DAY-TO-DAY LIFE

Talks by

Swami Krishnanand Saraswati

Edited by

Sylvia Arnold

ELEMENT BOOKS

© Sylvia Arnold 1988

First published 1983

This edition first published in Great Britain in 1988 by
Element Books Limited
Longmead, Shaftesbury, Dorset

Printed and bound in Great Britain by
Billings, Hylton Road, Worcester

Cover design by Ariane Dixon

Cover illustration by permission of the British Library

British Library Cataloguing in Publication Data
Krishnanand Saraswati, *Swami*
The Bhagavad-Gita in day-to-day life.
1. Hinduism. Bhagavad-gita : Expositions.
I. Title II. Arnold, Sylvia
294.5' 924

ISBN 1-85230-044-2

Contents

Foreword   I

Introduction   4

1. What is the *Bhagavad-Gita?*   12

    History of the *Gita*
    Its influence in modern times
    What *Bhagavad-Gita* gives to the seeker
    The problem of the *Gita (Gita* I)

2. The Teaching in a Nutshell *(Gita* II)   19

    The three basic principles
    Svadharma: The path of individual duty
    The right attitude
    Steadfast wisdom

3. Karma-Yoga, or the Path of Action *(Gita* III–VI)   36

    Various steps of action
    Action and non-action
    The key-principle: Control of the mind

4. Bhakti-Yoga, or the Path of Devotion *(Gita* VII–XII)   47

    Four kinds of devotees
    Death is the greatest guru
    The royal road
    One in All
    All in One
    Name and form: the right beginning

CONTENTS

5. Jnana-Yoga, or the Path of Knowledge   59
   (Gita XIII–XV*)*

   The relation between man and God
   The nature of man
   Completeness of knowledge

6. More Advice *(Gita* XVI and XVII*)*   65

   Good and evil – the conflict between divine
   and demonic tendencies
   Living in harmony

7. Summing Up *(Gita* XVIII*)*   69

   Notes and Glossary   71

Foreword

In 1975 I spent more than two months with Swami Krishnanand in Durban. His main object there was to teach young Indians about their cultural heritage, but he also gave a short lecture on the *Gita* every morning to an audience of three to eight people. I tape-recorded and then typed each lesson for the benefit of those present; there was no intention of publishing them, and only later did the idea come to us that one might edit the talks for a wider circle. I felt this to be a worthwhile task, the more so as Swami Krishnanand himself has, so far, not written any books about his teachings. At a time when the individual is so often encouraged to blame all his ills on shortcomings in his upbringing and on society at large, it may be helpful to remember the old ideals of self-control, devoted work, and surrender to God, which, according to the *Gita*, are the foundations for inner progress and for happiness in this as well as in the next life, practicable not only for monks, but for men and women living a full and active life.

The intention is not to add one more commentary on the *Gita* to the many that already exist, but to make accessible those aspects of the venerable book which have given help for right living to innumerable generations of Indians and can continue to give inspiration to people of our time in every part of the world. Swamiji's own introduction in chapter one will show this more clearly.

In Durban, South Africans of European as well as of Indian descent, Hindus and Christians, young and old, highly educated and more simple people, followed with rapt attention the talks by which Swamiji opened to all of us the riches of this heritage in a simple yet most fascinating way. Difficult notions and terms particular to Indian philosophy have been avoided wherever possible, because Swami Krishnanand holds that most of them are unnecessary for a right understanding of the essential teaching. In other words, the reader should not expect a full rendering or even a sort of digest of the *Gita*, but rather a guide to those parts which can teach us how to live a good life and die a good death even in our present dark age.

I have endeavoured to render these talks in a form that shall be understandable even for those who do not know the *Gita* as yet, hoping that it will tell the reader what it is all about and at the same time encourage him to read that priceless gift of India to the spiritual values of mankind. The best thing would be, of course, to study any of the several good translations together with the reading of our booklet. This was the procedure for the talks; as for the quotations in this book, they are taken from various translations (Sivananda, Radhakrishnan, and that by Swami Prabhavananda together with Christopher Isherwood).

The task I set myself has not been an easy one and I must apologize for my shortcomings. Talking and writing are two very different things, and Swami Krishnanand's lively and picturesque way of speaking loses much of its spontaneity when forced into the written word. Moreover, he always adapts his explanations to the understanding capacity of those present, and as there was much coming and going in our little circle the presentation varied from day to day. I have tried to put down the gist of Swamiji's talks, sometimes supplementing it from what he has said on other occasions, or asking him for additional explanation. I have endeavoured to let his wonderful sense of humour shine through here and there, and have incorporated some of the exemplifying stories – some his own, but mostly from the inexhaustible riches of Indian lore – with which he enlivened his talks in true oriental fashion. Neither have I cut out all the practical advice given to his listeners, even if not always in direct relation to the text of the *Gita*. In the Notes and Glossary at the end of the book, I have explained some Indian expressions and tried to give additional information where it seemed desirable. Sanskrit terms have been transcribed according to English pronunciation.

Swami Krishnanand has developed his own, in many ways unique, interpretation of the *Gita*, great in its simplicity. Naturally, his own convictions, his own way of life, have had their impact on his explanations. That is why I thought it fit to begin with a brief portrait of his remarkable personality, in order to make the reader appreciate the background against which one should understand this interpretation. Unfortunately, this portrait is incomplete, as Swamiji has cut out all that I had written about his birth, his education and earlier activities. "When one becomes a Swami, the past must be forgotten" he said. I am, however, grateful to him for having gone through the whole manuscript and for permitting me to have it published.

I wish to thank all those who have helped me to produce this book, particularly Professor Dr. Britta M. Charleston for putting my defective English into an acceptable form. May it add to our understanding of India's age-old wisdom, so helpful to many for mastering the problems of day-to-day life.

July 1983
Berne, Switzerland   SYLVIA ARNOLD

Introduction

The sun was setting over the Ruzizi valley. Violet shadows crept up the Congolese mountain range, while to the east the distant hills of Rwanda still glowed in the golden evening light.

Suddenly, the noise of an engine silenced the humming of the wilderness. From the veranda, I saw a car driving up to our solitary cottage, a cloud of red dust behind it. Out stepped a few Indians, merchants from Usumbura, and in their midst an ochre-clad Hindu monk. In surprise, I folded my hands in an Indian gesture of respect. A hearty laugh from the Swami:[1] "This is the first time a European lady has greeted me with Namaste in the middle of the African bush!"

Thus began, on June 17th, 1958, near the eastern border of the then Belgian Congo, a life-long association. What am I to call it? Swami Krishnanand was to teach me much that has deeply influenced my life, but if I say he became my guru,[2] you will associate him with those Indian "gurus" who are roaming the world making money. But he does not consider himself a guru, and he never accepts money: "I think that the moment money comes in, spiritual teaching becomes blurred by materialism. Moreover, there is one thing I am very much afraid of, and that is the ego of a guru. So I accept people, not as my disciples, but as my children, trying to guide them. Yet I never pretend that mine is the one and only correct way. I simply encourage people to bring up the good qualities that lie in every human being, and to avoid seeing bad things in others, because whatever we concentrate upon becomes ours – whether good or bad."

Children will provide their father with shelter, food, clothing and whatever else he may need, but never pay him a fee for his services and his teaching. Thus Swami Krishnanand

4

adheres strictly to his vows as a monk, without worldly possessions except a change of clothes and a few books, ever on the move among the members of his "family" spread far and wide over the world. They treat him with love and respect, but there is nothing of the cult and external adoration so often observed with India's "holy men", at home and abroad. The lean figure seems ageless, the keen eyes and the noble features radiate goodness and spirituality. A great gift for immediate contact with people of all walks of life and a fabulous memory convey the feeling, at each fresh meeting with him, even after several years, that the separation has never been real. He has a fine sense of humour and is full of spontaneity, yet you always feel his very great self-discipline, fruit of a yogic[3] way of life.

He was born in 1900 in what was then Jodhpur State (Rajasthan). A successful professional career seemed to give him everything that a young man could wish for. But this mundane life could not give satisfaction to one who has always felt a strong attraction to things spiritual. Over the years, this yearning grew more powerful; a painful event made him change his way of life gradually to that of a renunciate. He found his guru and took up in earnest the study of the old scriptures and the practice of yoga. At the age of 37 he was ordained into an age-old, highly reputed monastery at Rishikesh.[4]

"But I had not become a sannyasin[5] to do nothing", he recalls. When he was rebuked one day for having rushed out of his cell to separate some lepers who were fighting, and taking one of them, badly injured, to hospital, instead of ignoring his cries for help and remaining concentrated on his studies, he told the head of the monastery: "Shankaracharya[6] taught that God is in all and every thing, hence true practice of Vedanta[7] means love for all men. In the given situation, this forced me to act." And he left, not the ideals and the way of life of a Sannyasin, but the monastery walls, realizing that for him, who from childhood had felt in his compassionate heart the urge to help suffering human beings, religion and service must be one.

It was in 1950 that his wanderings abroad began. In Nepal,

Sikkim, Bhutan and Tibet, he became instrumental in establishing libraries, dispensaries, etc.; his initiative in the field of relief to the blind made him known in parts of these Himalayan countries as "the Swami who gives sight". Yet "It was not I, but the doctors who, by the grace of God, gave eyesight", Swamiji[8] says. "What these simple people felt and expressed is that work of that kind can only be done when someone sets it in motion. I can help only through the hands of those whose hearts I convince that they can – and must – help."

When he was back in India, he met several East Africans of Indian descent. They all told him about the large Indian communities in those countries and spoke of their great need of spiritual guidance, inviting him to come and do something for them. Thus began one of the most important chapters in Swami Krishnanand's life: in the autumn of 1956 he landed in Mombasa.

It was not an easy task in the beginning. "Most of these people had come from India to earn a livelihood. Now they had businesses, houses, all kinds of comforts. But people without a strong cultural basis easily become intoxicated by money, by success . . . the old values had almost been lost . . . they had become barren and dry within, and very unhappy . . . happiness lies in human, in divine, values, and so I first of all began my work in the cultural field."[9]

Through his "*Gita Society*" in Nairobi, hundreds of young people learned from this wonderful book. To foster unity in the families, he encouraged them to sing, pray, and read together from India's holy scriptures for at least half an hour every day. Wherever he went in East Africa (and, in the course of time, in most of the countries of that continent), he made a point of visiting all the various Indian communities, encouraging them to preserve their cultural values, but not in a sectarian way. "Think of yourselves as citizens of the world. There is only one race, and that is the human race. Live creditably wherever you have been placed by God's will and remember Gandhiji's motto: 'Service to man is service to God.'"

It was in 1960 that my husband and I experienced Swami Krishnanand's great readiness and capacity for service. When he heard over the radio the news of the troubles that had broken out in the Congo, only a few days after Independence, he rushed from Lake Victoria to Lake Kivu, where we were then living. When he arrived, United Nations troops were patrolling the streets of Bukavu and many white people had already left. He asked some Indians from neighbouring Ruanda-Urundi (then still under Belgian rule) to buy our furniture and change our Congo francs, which had lost all value, into East African shillings, in order to help prepare for our departure. Swamiji left with us the once beautiful town, now shaken by insecurity and fear. In Usumbura (now Bujumbura), we made final preparations in view of our departure for Ceylon (Sri Lanka), where my husband had luckily obtained a post. Swamiji went on ahead down Lake Tanganyika by passenger boat, smiling: "Hanuman must now go and prepare the way to Lanka!" [10]

And he did so. When, after a stormy passage, we arrived at the entrance of Port Kigoma with our little cabin cruiser, some Indians waved to us, showing us where to berth, offering us hospitality and the medical care of which I was in need. They saw to it that our boat was loaded on to the train for Dar-es-Salaam, and when we arrived there ourselves, one day in the small hours of the morning (Swamiji having travelled with us as far as Tabora), a young Indian couple welcomed us on the platform: "Please come with us, your room is ready." In our difficult situation, the material side of all this was very welcome, but what impressed us more deeply was this sympathy and kindness irrespective of creed and colour. It was the first, but not the last, time that I had reason to marvel at the amount of goodwill a word, even a glance from Swami Krishnanand can rouse in people. Yet never have I seen him use this power for egoistic purposes; to help others, and to induce others to help, is all he has in mind. This attitude was to become even more determining for his activities during his later stay in Africa, from where he had returned to India shortly after our own departure.

It was then that life in large parts of Asia was paralyzed by a constellation of the stars considered extremely unlucky; for days, 'planes and trains travelled almost empty. Swami

Krishnanand seized the opportunity, by travelling in a special train with some 400 of his friends the length and breadth of India, to demonstrate that such fear is unwarranted, because our lives are governed by God and not by the stars.

This incident stands here for many others to illustrate Swamiji's independent thinking – which, I am sure, must often have baffled and angered the fundamentalists among his fellow-countrymen. Yet Swami Krishnanand considers himself faithful to tradition – not to superstition and rigidity, but to tradition as "a foundation on which we have to establish progress."

1963 saw him start on a world tour undertaken with the aim of learning how welfare work is organized in other countries. This certainly helped him in his further activities, first in India (organization of "eye camps" where hundreds of poor blind patients were operated on and treated, of dispensaries and educational institutions), then in Africa. Arriving at Nairobi airport in 1965, he told the friends who had come to greet him that this time he had not come to spread God's name, but to do God's work.

One day later, Machakos district was declared a famine area, and when Swami Krishnanand expressed his wish to start relief work, it became clear that, despite many failures, part of the seed sown during Swamiji's first stay in Africa had come up. Many Indians finally understood what he had told them again and again, namely, that they had duties not only towards their own community but to their country of adoption and all its inhabitants. His *Gita* – and Satsang [11] groups now became the basis for the collection and distribution of food and other necessities, feeding many thousand people daily.

It was not long before many of these Indians were to be in need of help themselves. Swamiji found them begging in front of the temples in Nairobi, because the Kenya Government's new "Work Permit Law" no longer allowed them to work and they had nowhere else to go. In these difficult times "Deen Bandhu Samaj" [12] was founded, and although there were no funds in the beginning, this organization was soon doing very efficient work. When I visited them ten years later, I found them still active, helping Indians to obtain the necessary papers

8

for emigration to India or to Great Britain, feeding and clothing poor Indians and Africans – and even stranded Europeans. While I was there, they received, for the first time, a donation from a Christian Mission, a gesture which – modest though it was – moved these workers very deeply. It was for them a token of trust and respect, coming as it did from a source which they could hardly have expected to support them.

A similar organization was started in Uganda, concentrating its assistance to organizations founded by others (Missions, etc.) for the benefit of Africans – leprosaria, orphanages, rehabilitation centres for blind people, etc. In Zambia, the "Human Service Society" (a name later also given to organizations outside Africa) was the first to have members of all races and all religions united in the conviction that "service to man is service to God".

The list of humanitarian activities that Swami Krishnanand has set in motion in a great many countries could be extended yet further.

Since 1972 he has spent much time in Great Britain, where thousands of former East African Indians are now living and where his "Human Service Trust" is active in various fields. But he also pays visits to "his children" on the Continent, in Africa, North America, the Middle East and South East Asia. During his sojourns in India, the training of social workers and the organization of blind relief work are among his main activities.

Swami Krishnanand has often watched Christian Missionaries in their humanitarian activities in the slums of Bombay, as well as in the African bush. He does not hesitate to praise them to his Indian listeners for their "work done for the love of God". Back in India, I once met a Swami of a modern order who told me that the time was past for Sannyasins to walk about with their begging bowl and that it was their duty to help the poor instead of eating their meagre food. And he added: "We learnt that from the Christian missionaries." When I told Swami Krishnanand about this, he quickly agreed: "They have brought back to us the awareness of something which, in India, had been narrowed down by casteism [13] and by ritualism. But compassion, generosity, and unselfish service being in no way alien to our own scriptures and ideals, we can follow this path without any conversion."

He dislikes proselytizing in others, and he does not do so himself. That I, as his "child", should live up better to the teachings of Christ is all he expects from me. One day, I accompanied him on a visit to the Bishop of Las Palmas (Canary Islands), with whom he had appeared on TV to ask the Spanish people's help for the (mostly Muslim) flood victims in Bangladesh; never shall I forget the mutual esteem and understanding between the two men. The Bishop enquired about life in a Hindu monastery, and about yoga. "Each effort to reach unity with God is a form of yoga", he was told, "Catholicism practised in daily life not excluded". At parting, they embraced, the man in black with a violet cap nodding assent to the ochre-clad monk's words: "Let us praise God in any of His many names!" On our return drive Swamiji remarked: "Exactly the same questions were asked by the Pope when I saw him in 1963, and he received the same answers." It is only in such a casual way that he talks of his meetings with many great men of this world. When President Kennedy asked him what he thought of the American aid to India, he asked in return: "What are the intentions behind that aid? I ask this question because it is the intention that determines the action." And smilingly he recalls: "The President was even more baffled when I told him that they ought to speak their own language in America – and not talk of their western neighbours as of 'the East'!"

Swami Krishnanand has great respect for all religions and is convinced that each of them has given something important to the world. "What made them grow and survive? With Hinduism it has been its spiritual nature, with Islam brotherhood, and with Christianity service to one's fellow men. But in our day no religion can remain a potent force if it emphasises one of these aspects at the expense of another. If you take water out of a block of ice, what remains? The block? Or nothing? So Christianity must regain spirituality, Hinduism the ideal of service to man, if they are to survive."

"Service", for Swamiji, covers a wide ground, from food for the starving to spiritual guidance to the seeker. And he will give such aid according to the nature of an individual. The intellectual will be encouraged to study – and Swami Krishnanand himself is always eager to read and learn. But he does not think much of teaching philosophical theories for their own sake, insisting rather on their aspect as a help to right living. Therefore, in his talks, he always bears in mind the type of audience he has before him and never shows the great scholar he is. "I feel that my duty does not lie in the first place with intellectuals, but I must go to the masses and take to them a philosophy that inspires and encourages them to develop all that is good within them. My experiences in Asia, in Africa and in Europe have convinced me that the *Gita* can actually help in this way. I do not base my talks on the commentaries of the great masters of the past, but try to give my own commentary adapted to our time. Like Gandhi and Vinobaji [14], I call *Gita* my mother, because it gives me a mother's guidance – and when I talk about the *Gita*, it comes from the very depth of my heart."

S.A.

I

What is the *Bhagavad–Gita?*

How often, my dear friends, has this little book which I always carry with me and about which I am going to talk to you, given me inspiration in difficult situations! It is not for nothing that it is so extremely popular in India. Some people know all its 18 chapters by heart, and many want to hear it on their death-bed. In my talks, I shall endeavour to offer you a simple interpretation of the main aspects of this wonderful book – not a highly philosophical one, but one that may help you in everyday life. I am not going to interpret it shloka by shloka, verse by verse, but shall try to convey to you the essence of the meaning which each section has for our present age, and show how we can realize its teaching in our own lives.

We are a small group. Some of you are Westerners, and those with Indian names and faces were born and brought up far away from India, in a foreign land. I shall therefore speak to you in a way that can be understood without much knowledge of Indian tradition by those living in the world of to-day. We must concentrate on essential aspects, but after understanding these, I am confident that you will be able to understand even those parts of the *Gita* which may at first seem obscure. Just bear in mind that this book brings abstract, spiritual knowledge clothed in pictures and similes easily accessible to Indians who lived thousands of years ago, and then you can endeavour to find out the message that these pictures and similes are intended to convey, translated into the language of our own day.

History of the Gita

The 700 verses of the *Gita* are inserted in the 6th Canto of the *Mahabharata*, one of the two great epics of India. Both of them, the *Mahabharata* and the *Ramayana*, are among the

12

earliest known epic poems of mankind. Yet in spite of their venerable age, they are not dead literature. People in India live with them, because they embody the philosophy of the *Vedas*, *popular* giving guidance for right living in the attractive form of story and dialogue, easily understandable to highly educated and illiterate people alike.

According to traditional belief, Vyasa, the legendary author of the *Mahabharata*, also wrote the *Puranas* and the *Brahma Sutras*. This may or may not be so; in any case the *Gita* gives the essence of all the thinking expressed in these books. Just as the whole tree is contained in a small seed, so the whole of Indian philosophy may be found in the *Gita*. It is difficult to *Summary* say when the *Gita* was written. For Indians this is not important, because in our opinion it is "important to eat the fruit and not to count the trees". [15]

The *Gita* has, in its present form, deeply influenced Indian thinking for hundreds of generations. The Masters of the various schools of Vedantic thought have commented on it, and it is a corner-stone of Indian culture. Krishna is the most beloved divine name to the masses, and they take Gita as his message. Hence the name "*Bhagavad–Gita*", the song of God.

After the decay of Muslim rule, during which the living forces of Indian tradition had been suppressed, leaving only the rigid forms of rituals and casteism [13], and under the impact of western influence, reformist movements such as the Arya Samaj and the Brahmo Samaj brought a new assessment of our own heritage. It was Vivekananda who, influenced by his great spiritual Master, Ramakrishna, revealed anew the greatness of the *Bhagavad–Gita*, valid through all the ages and for all people. Vivekananda also made the *Gita* known to the western world, but he was not the first to do so. Can we consider it to be mere coincidence that the *Gita* was the first work of Indian philosophy to be translated directly from the Sanskrit into a European language (Charles Wilkins, 1785), and not, as was the case with other scriptures, from a Persian translation? The book greatly impressed European thinkers of the 18th and 19th centuries, particularly German philosophers such as Hegel and Schopenhauer. And it was none other than Warren Hastings, first Governor General of India, who, in an introduction to Wilkins' translation, wrote that the *Gita* would live "when the British dominion in India shall have long ceased to exist and when the sources which it once yielded to wealth and power are lost to remembrance." [16]

Its influence in modern times

What Warren Hastings could hardly foresee was the great role the *Gita* was to play in the Liberation Movement which brought this "British dominion in India" to an end. Revolutionaries used to go to their execution reciting verses from the holy book, such as:

> *Not wounded by weapons,*
> *not burned by fire,*
> *not dried by the wind,*
> *not wetted by water:*
> *Such is the Atman.*

(Chapter II, shloka, or verse, 23.)

Aurobindo, Tilak and Gandhi cited this sacred book and commented on it, and that is why people understood and followed them. During the struggle for independence, Vinoba Bhave, the great spiritual heir of Mahatma Gandhi (known to the West particularly through his "Bhoodan" or "Land-for-the-landless-movement" in the 'fifties) gave a series of eighteen lectures to his fellow-prisoners, and these have been published in more than a million copies in most of the Indian languages, as well as in many others, with the title *Talks on the Gita*. This book made people realize the significance and the meaning of this age-old wisdom for modern man. But circumstances change continually, and so interpretation, too, must change. It is quite possible that Vinoba, and even Gandhi, would explain certain things differently to-day from the way they did during the struggle for independence.

What Bhagavad—Gita gives to the seeker

Not only must the *Gita* be explained anew for each period, but also interpreted according to the understanding of a given type of people. Indians will understand it against the background of

Indian tradition; replace the Indian background by intelligent interpretation, and you will find that this wonderful heritage is for the West, too. The reason is that the *Gita* inspires each individual to find his own path to salvation. This explains why the most diverse schools of thought accept it as one of the three pillars of Indian philosophy [17], and why non-Indians also find their convictions confirmed by it. Even nihilists and atheists accept the *Gita* as a book of inspiration. To do one's duty in life free from selfishness is, according to the *Gita*, of no lesser value than to renounce the world. Also, to realize God as the one life-force which transcends the whole of creation leads to the same goal as to worship Him in the form of a personal God, under any of His many names. The *Gita* helps everyone to strengthen his own way of progress. To those who understand this, there is no need for any conversion. Lord Krishna says: "It matters not what deity a devotee chooses to worship. If he has faith, I make his faith unwavering" (VII, 21). Add to this generous tolerance the noble and poetic language of the *Gita*, the lively dialogue in which it explains the problems of life and their solutions – and you will understand why it has become, and remained, the most popular of all Indian holy scriptures.

In most other religious teachings, there is little room for questioning; belief is stressed as the first necessity. This makes it difficult for modern man to keep his traditional faith alive, and he turns to philosophy, where he is free to question. In India, we do not make this difference, we see no antagonism between religion and philosophy, as we consider that conviction must come before faith. From your Western angle, it is better to consider the *Bhagavad–Gita* as a book of philosophy rather than as one of religion. This will keep you from making yourselves victims of blind faith. Here, as in everything, blind faith blocks progress. The real seeker must question, and go on questioning. From each answer there arises a new question, and so the individual develops, step by step. It is precisely this process of evolution through continuous questioning that the *Gita* unfolds before us.

15

The problem of the Gita (Gita 1)

The central theme of the *Mahabharata*, this grandiose poem of about 100,000 verses, is the conflict between two branches of the descendants of King Bharata: the Pandavas, who are the five sons of Pandu, and the Kauravas, the hundred sons of Pandu's half-brother, blind King Dhritarashtra. It is a thrilling story of human weakness as well as of noble acts, full of wisdom in many of its chapters, using the picture of a cruel war in order to illustrate the battle between Good and Evil that man has to fight. One special aspect of this fight, the clash between conflicting duties, is shown in the *Gita*. materialism + spiritualism

The opposing armies of the Pandavas and the Kauravas are drawn up for the decisive battle when the blind King Dhritarashtra asks his Minister Sanjaya: "What did my people and the sons of Pandu do when they had gathered on the holy field of Kurukshetra, eager for battle?" *(1, 1)*.

With this question begins the *Bhagavad—Gita*, in the middle of the *Mahabharata*. Sanjaya is gifted with clairvoyance and clairaudience, which enables him to describe to his King everything he sees and hears on the distant plain of Kurukshetra. King Dhritarashtra speaks only once, when he asks the opening question. In fact, the whole narrative of the *Gita* is Sanjaya's answer to that question. He describes to the blind King how his son Duryodhana, leader of the Kauravas, enumerates to his teacher Drona the famous kings and heroes who have come from all over the country to the help of one or other of the two parties.

Then Sanjaya's eyes fall upon Arjuna, the leader of the Pandavas, and Krishna, his charioteer, who are standing in their chariot drawn by white horses and blowing their conches. Amidst the tremendous noise of conches and kettledrums, of tabors, drums and cowhorns that announce the beginning of the battle, Arjuna requests his charioteer to drive the chariot between the two armies so that he may see those he must fight.

Arjuna is a mighty and peerless hero, master of the art of warfare, but at the same time a peace-loving man of noble character. And who is Krishna? He speaks to Arjuna first as his friend, then as God. In other words: Krishna is the immortal Divine in man, the Atman [18], talking to Arjuna, the mind. At the very moment the battle is to begin, they engage in the conversation which is recorded in the *Bhagavad–Gita*. We thus have two couples: Krishna and Arjuna on the battlefield, Dhritarashtra and Sanjaya in the palace at Hastinapur (Delhi).

Jealousy and greed on the part of the Kauravas have made war inevitable. As has been narrated in the previous chapter of the *Mahabharata*, all efforts for a peaceful solution have been in vain, Duryodhana having refused the offer of an honourable settlement, letting them understand clearly that he would rather destroy the Pandavas than give back even a "needle-point" of the territory won from King Yuddhistira, the eldest son of the Pandavas, while gambling. But although his army has eleven divisions against seven of the Pandavas, Duryodhana is afraid of his cousins. Like everyone else on the battlefield, he knows that they have every chance of winning, because Arjuna is the greatest hero of their time and because they are fighting for a just cause.

Arjuna is also aware of this, and the possibility of victory or fear of defeat does not worry him. But his mind is torn with grief at this tragic war between near relatives, and by doubts concerning his seemingly conflicting duties. Is it right for him to fight against his kinsmen, even to kill them, just because he knows that his side is in the right and they are in the wrong? Would it not be better to spare his relatives, his dearest grandfather and his beloved guru, who had taught him everything? Where does his duty lie?

Duryodhana, on the other hand, is Arjuna's opposite in every respect. He is not troubled with conflicting duties, but with the choice between good and evil. Yet, he never asks himself about the righteousness of his cause; it is not that he does not know the difference between right and wrong, but he just cannot desist from Evil.

The *Gita* is not concerned with Duryodhana, but with the problem of Arjuna who, in this great war between good and evil, stands on the side of righteousness. For him, the choice between good and evil was made long ago, but he now has to choose between two ways that seem to him equally good. This is Arjuna's problem, explained at the beginning of the *Gita* up to Chapter II, 10.

Arjuna's problem is every good person's problem. Situations often arise that leave a choice between two morally justifiable but contradictory courses of action. Such perplexing situations confront only the honest man: the dishonest ones are guided solely by their own desires, their self-interest. But desires and self-interest are not always easily recognizable as such. Take the choice that Arjuna has to make. Even though he knows that the fruit of victory, the kingdom, will fall to his eldest brother and not to himself, he asks: is it not selfish to take one's own path just because it is right? Would it not, on the other hand, be an unselfish act to do good to people who are doing wrong to me and my brothers?

To teach Arjuna to find a way out of this confusing situation, to lead him from despondency to firmness, is the object and essence of Krishna's teaching. It is not a fight between armies, between men, that we are going to witness, but a fight within man. Arjuna symbolizes the mind, sitting in the chariot – the body – together with Krishna, the Atman, the real Self. Sanjay is the intellect, which records objectively and transmits all he sees and hears; only at the end of his narrative (XVIII, 74–78) does he express his own judgment. The horses symbolize the senses, the reins their control. Kurukshetra, the battlefield, is this world of outer contradiction as well as inner conflicts and weaknesses which man must overcome.

2

The Teaching in a Nutshell
(Gita II)

"Place my Chariot between the two armies, that I may see those who stand here desirous to fight!" (1, 21) Why does Arjuna give this order to his charioteer? Although he had previously handed over the reins of the chariot, that is, the control of the senses to the charioteer, the Atman, even this noble mind succumbs to curiosity. Arjuna moves away from the side of right and closer to the side of evil. And now, seeing the familiar faces of relatives and teachers, he who was perfectly at ease so long as he remained on the side of right, suddenly sees his path divide into two [19]. He becomes uncertain, he is in a dilemma, he weeps and groans – and even starts arguing with his charioteer: Mind is in conflict with Atman, and Atman has to labour very hard to convince him.

At first, Krishna scolds Arjuna in severe words and admonishes him to shake off his disgraceful cowardice. It is not at such a decisive hour, when the task that must be done is imminent, that man can start pondering about his duty! But Arjuna is in a very deep and violent crisis. What he had till then regarded as his unquestionable and natural duty, has suddenly become sinful to his mind. He implores Krishna to help him, to tell him what he must do: Mind asks God within for guidance. This is a first step in the right direction, but by adding: "I will not fight", Arjuna at the same time shows that he is not yet really ready to follow the advice he is asking for. Krishna helps him in fact, not by giving an order or making a decision for him, but by explaining to him that supreme knowledge which will help him to make his own decisions, not only in his present conflict, but forever. Gradually, we see Arjuna being led from ignorance to knowledge, from darkness to light, from physical consciousness to spiritual consciousness.

19

Only then has Atman won over Mind, making it powerful and good at the same time. As long as Mind succumbs to its own desires and goes against the will of God, it is unhappy, depressed and weak. Mind must listen to the supreme soul within and obey Atman. But Atman never speaks; he uses a herald, an interpreter, to express and explain the divine language to Mind. This interpreter is our faculty of mental understanding and intuitive spiritual discernment, which we usually call the intellect. [20]

But Mind also receives impressions from the outside world, conveyed to it by the senses. It is for the mind, the intelligent will, to decide what to do: to listen to the senses and become totally engulfed in the outside world, or to turn its attention inwards, where it can hear the divine voice, as soon as the influence of the senses is excluded – just as the ticking of a clock can be heard only when the noise from outside stops.

We can think of the Atman as of a lamp shining within, under the transparent covering of the mind. The senses are the second covering, the world outside the third. Without the shining light of the Atman, the mind, senses and outside world would all be only darkness. Mind is capable of realizing the existence of the Divine within, and an enlightened mind turns inward to where the light shines. Only ignorance makes a mind believe that the light which falls, through him, upon the outside world, is his own, forgetting that it is only a "borrowed" light. When the mind is not aware of the fact that it lives and functions only through the Atman, when it turns to the outer world and says "I am the thinker, I am the doer", it is doing a wrong and dangerous thing. Mind must turn inward and stand humbly, with folded hands, before the Atman, receiving and obeying his command. Only then does it find the real happiness that comes from within, and is freed from the unhappiness that comes entirely from the world outside.

It is not easy for Mind to learn this. Only at the end of the *Gita*, when the teaching is completed, are Arjuna's doubts ended, dead for ever. Only now is the control of actions permanently handed over to the Atman; Atman and Mind walk together, hand in hand, and the *Gita* ends with Sanjaya's words:

20

Where Lord Krishna is, and Arjuna,
great among archers,
There, I know, is goodness and peace,
and triumph and glory!

(XVIII, 78)

All eighteen chapters are important for helping you to reach this unity of Mind with Atman. The second, however, gives the basis for understanding them all. If it is too much for you to manage the whole book, make a careful study (and practice) of the second chapter only, and it will help you to conquer the delusions of ignorance which veil the vision of your path. It is, as it were, the *Gita* in a nutshell. The chapters that follow may be regarded as interpretations. Chapters III–VI give detailed instructions for Karma-yoga, or the path of action, chapters VII–XII for Bhakti-yoga, or the path of devotion, chapters XIII–XV for Jnana-yoga, or the path of knowledge. Chapters XVI and XVII give additional explanations, and in chapter XVIII, the whole of the *Gita* is summed up.

"Yoga" is the way by which the principles and the ideals developed in the *Gita* can be put into practice. The different yogas are complementary to each other, and there is no strict division between them. Practised in absolute sincerity and honesty, they all lead to the same goal. It depends on your nature, which of them appeals to you most.

In the second chapter, the divine teacher explains to his disciple three things: the nature of the physical body, that of Atman, the eternal Self, and of action that leads man to awareness, to the realization of his Self. In its last eighteen verses, he draws a concise picture of one who has reached such awareness and lives accordingly. He is the ideal man, the man of steadfast wisdom, who has reached the highest goal shown to us in such a magnificent way in the *Bhagavad–Gita*.

The three basic principles
— The body is mortal
— Atman, the Divine in man, is immortal, eternal, all-pervading
— as long as Atman and the body are together, activity is natural and inevitable.

In these dry sentences we may summarize what the *Gita* expresses in beautiful verses, developing at the same time the consequences to be drawn from these basic facts of life. *(*II, 11–53*)* We all know that our physical body is mortal, starting its march towards death from the moment it is born. Nobody knows when that final moment will come for him.

And yet, when we say "I", we usually think of this mortal body of ours. Am "I", then, something that changes every day? For this is what the body does. Can you recognize in an old man the child he once was? What we call the death of the body is also change – it changes into dust, and out of the dust will grow food for another body.

No – the reality of my "I" is not this ever-changing matter, not the body with its sensations of pleasure and pain. "I" am not eyes, not ears, not hands, not tongue – "I" am that power which makes my eyes see, my ears hear, my hands work, my tongue talk. That which permeates the living body is immortal. It is Atman, the real Self, the innermost soul, which is one with Brahman, the life-force that pervades the entire universe. Those who have realized this do not worry about the inevitable change and death of the body, but remain conscious of their own divine nature, and that of others. To differentiate between the mortal ego and the real Self which transcends the body and which cannot become diseased, grow old or be killed: this is life's purpose.

The way to the true realization of the Self is long, and human life is very short – too short, in our opinion, to go the full length of the way to realization. According to the Indian view, man[21] is born again and again in a new body, till he achieves perfection, that is, truly realizes the Self. Then only is liberation from the cycle of births and deaths attained. For those who do not accept this view and who think that paradise

must be won in one life only, the fact becomes even m[ore]
pressing that man can act only in the time given him, in the
given body. Belief in some form of existence after death is
inherent in all religions, but even those who do not believe in
anything of that kind at all, feel that they must make the best
use of their lives. We have no scientific proof as to which belief
is right. But we all know that we have been given a body and
the capacity to do something, in the given time. Accept this
fact gladly, and use your energy, your body, your lifespan, as
well as the good qualities God has blessed you with, to the best
possible purpose. You are free to misuse God's gifts, but by
doing so you miss life's happiness and purpose: to realize God
within you, that is your Self, the all-pervading Atman.

From the moment the Divine, Atman, takes its place in
a body, activity starts, and goes on as long as the two stay
together. This is true for all creatures. But only man is able to
become aware of his divine nature and to differentiate between
good and evil actions. This is what distinguishes the human
from all other beings. Therefore, the great question "Who am
I?" must first be understood. It is the centre of the teachings of
the *Gita*. Once this is realized, all the answers come from your
own Self – and there is "no need to be drowned in the oceans of
Rama and Krishna, Buddha and Jesus Christ – keep your head
above the waters and swim!" (Swami Ramtirth)

Svadharma: The path of individual duty

The *Gita* emphasizes the fact that what is right for one person
may be wrong for another, for the actions of an individual
must correspond to the duty that he has to perform in life. This
duty is called svadharma. "Sva" means "own", "dharma"
may be translated by "law", "duty", or by "factors ruling
existence". So "svadharma" is the law of my own life, the
factors that rule it. It is the God-given path on which an individual can progress.

The divine teacher reminds Arjuna of the high ideals and the
code of honour pertaining to his position in life. They are
the moral values he has been taught to consider as the law of
his own nature, and he cannot give them up without doing
great harm to himself. Therefore he must fight [22].

Family traditions and upbringing naturally influence every-body's svadharma. Whether his conditions of birth are the result of an individual's deeds in previous lives, or whether you accept the obvious inequalities of people's starting chances in life as God-given, this much remains certain: there are, for every individual, a number of given facts, of conditions he must accept. We cannot choose the time and place of our birth, our parents or the way in which they bring us up. We cannot change the colour of our skin or our temperament. Further-more, each individual has his deficiencies as well as his own natural gifts. One man may have a keen intellect, another a devotional or compassionate heart; one may be physically strong or a talented artist. All these given factors constitute the basis of our individual being. They make the warp of the cloth that is our life; the woof is the work, the energy, the endeavour we put into the weaving.

In other words: in order to develop, we must make use of the given framework. There is no such thing as high and low in this respect. The man who lives his own life in the right attitude, even under the most miserable conditions and with poor talents, can rise towards perfection and spiritual free-dom, whereas the one who misuses his worldly riches or his great intelligence egoistically and to the detriment of others, is far from realizing the divine purpose of life. You must find out for yourself where your svadharma lies. This may at times seem difficult, but it is really a quite natural thing. Ask your Self within. It answers when you call it, just as a person sitting in a room answers a call from outside. But unless the caller knows that somebody is there, he does not call – how then could there be an answer? So always be conscious of the Divine within yourself. Others may guide you to find your svadharma, but only by love and understanding, never by pressing their own view. To force one's view on someone else is very bad. Discover for yourself where your best talent lies, and then try to develop it. If you have received many talents, remember that progress comes through concentration on one of them, not through squandering the given life-span by running after too many things. Should you find, in the course of time, that you have made a mistake and must change your plans, swallow your pride and change them. Whenever a person awakens to his svadharma, life really starts.

Yet developing your talent is just one aspect of your svadharma; it is a means on the way to Self-realization, never an end in itself. I have been told that nowadays many people use the expression "self-realization" for the process of developing their individual talents as such and for leading an egoistic life. This has, of course, nothing to do with the Self-realization of the *Gita*. It is nothing but "ego-realization"! Egoism has no place in svadharma. Only what we do without any trace of selfishness, with a pure heart, completely surrendered to God, leads to real happiness and to the spiritual perfection we have set out to seek, and which culminates in the realization, the experience, the becoming aware of our true Self, of God within, Atman.

This is what Arjuna has to understand in the end: not by doing what he would prefer to do at this crucial moment, but by remaining firm, without any thought of the results for himself, adhering to the God-given task, can he fulfil his life's purpose. You can help yourself by accepting your Svadharma, or you can harm yourself by trying to evade it. There is no third way. *V 31-33*

It is very important to understand svadharma rightly. Indian lore abounds with stories by which sages and poets have explained it, again and again, as duty done without any thought of reward. A very instructive one is that of Pundalik, a simple man who is nursing his old parents. Outside, in the rainy night, Pandurang (a Maharashtrian name for Lord Krishna) calls him, standing in the water. But Pundalik only throws him a brick on which to stand and apologizes for not being able to do anything more for him at that moment. His duty lies in serving his parents, and this he does with all devotion, the name of God always in his heart. Pandurang is God, but to Pundalik, his parents are also God. He does not serve them with the intention of seeing Pandurang appear at his door. God will come wherever unselfish service is done in His name, but Pundalik is not asking for this, or any other reward.

A man with this kind of clear vision of his own svadharma

will also respect that of others, and he will not fall into the tangle of conflicting philosophies. Someone else may follow another principle, and to raise a controversy over which one is right, leads to nothing. Both ways may be right, but your way is not my way. Once you have found your path, follow it, do not let yourself be diverted.

Your qualities, your energy, your lifespan become manifest in your body. With all its God-given gifts, it is your tool for svadharma. Keep it clean and healthy, but do not identify yourself with the tool! Do not become attached to it! And when the time comes, discard it without fear, as you would a worn-out garment. Who, indeed, could wish to keep a weak, diseased body for ever? To perform exercises or to follow certain rules concerning food, can be very helpful in developing the body physically and as an instrument for inner progress. Yet instead of progressing, many people only become more body-minded by such practices. They confound the way with the goal, they become attached to the body as if it were their real Self. How can you use your intelligence, your artistic talent, your capacity to swim fast over a long distance, for svadharma, if you mistake all these bodily things for the Self and worship them as such?

Our lifespan is limited: we do not know its length, but it is certain that every hour brings us nearer to the end. Use the given time for svadharma, do not waste it. Svadharma changes in the course of time: in youth, it may mean hard studies, in later years, hard work. A time may come when all we are able to do is to bear the weaknesses of old age patiently and to give a smile to those who look after us: that also can be svadharma. And when the last hour comes, we leave without that guilty conscience which is the result of time wasted, of a wasted life.

The right attitude

After explaining in theory the true nature of man and his duty in life [23], Lord Krishna teaches us, through his pupil, the great art of giving each of the basic principles – Atman, body and action – its right place in life. This art, says Krishna, is called yoga. Yoga is part of our daily living, like breathing. You cannot practice it for a few minutes and then forget about it: it must be part of you and stay with you all the time. True, even a little effort will benefit you, says the *Gita* – but only when there is complete concentration on the Divine within, can you reach that union, that wonderful harmony between the natural life-forces.

Great powers are obtained by spiritual yoga, yet one who uses them for selfish ends may be a magician, but he is not a yogi. The true yogi does not want any of these powers for himself. He is dedicated to serving others. This he can never do by performing miracles; the only way to help others is to make things clear to them, so that they may find their own way. Miracles take man away from his own path and make him dependent upon the performer of miracles. Keep this in mind: never hanker after miracles! If somebody is helpful for your svadharma, listen to him – otherwise do not.

Man's actions are conditioned by the three gunas [24]: Laziness will not let him work – that is tamas. He is ready to work, but only if there is a reward – that is rajas. The man who works has a natural right to reward. But he who, working for duty's sake alone, does not think of reward, is prompted by sattva. He receives over and above the reward, a hundred times more in happiness. To act in this attitude, and to give up one's actions to the Lord, is sattva. This is what the *Gita* tells us to do. If we perform our duty in this spirit, all things in life will be helpful for our inner progress, just as every part of a bicycle becomes useful to one who knows how to ride it.

Man finds it difficult to achieve that kind of happiness because he attaches himself to material reward. Yet, if you plant a tree, and nurse it, fruit will come of its own accord – so why think of it, why hanker after it?

So long as there is attachment to material things, the goal of our life's journey cannot be reached: A man has walked for miles to visit a temple. When he gets there, he cannot make up his mind to take off his shoes, for fear they might be stolen. So he cannot enter the temple and remains standing outside. The man who stands outside the temple-door does not receive prasad [25]. The man who goes inside does receive prasad – but it is not for the sweets that he has come; they are only a material addition to the happiness he feels after his prayer. Happiness is very close the moment we renounce attachments!

Many people think that complete detachment is possible only by giving up all worldly activities and becoming a Sannyasin, a renunciate. The truth is that as long as you feel the warmth of your home, it is very difficult not to be attached to it. But if you run away from home, yet keep thinking of the things at home, where is the detachment of the mind? It is mere escapism – though even that can be helpful, in the beginning, for overcoming attachment. To become a sannyasin is like going to school: a student can learn at home also; going to school is not essential, but it makes learning easier!

Both ways, staying at home or running away, can lead to enlightenment – and both are full of temptations which may divert you from the real goal. Even the desire to have a vision of God can become a temptation, a great temptation. Suppose that, finally, after much austerity, hard exercises and month-long meditation, the miracle of such a vision occurs: it is just a flash – and then what? Such a man will be completely lost. But he who is aware of such temptations will do what brings God nearer to him (like Pundalik), and then stay near God, always.

Detached action alone gives purity of mind, thus removing the obstacles of desire and greed. In everyday practice, we must control, with sincerity and honesty, the motives that prompt our actions. "To unite the heart with Brahman and then to act: that is the secret of non-attached work" (II, 48). Stay near God always – and then do what you like! By keeping God always in mind, intentions are purified, and when the intentions are pure, even that which may look like a sin may be a good deed. It is not always possible to act without harming other creatures; even gardening and cooking result in the death of millions of microbes and many tiny animals. And it may happen that, with the best of intentions, you fail – but would you call the doctor a criminal if the patient whom he tried to save by an operation in an extreme situation dies? Or the guard who, in the dark, shoots a burglar, thus avoiding a bank-robbery? No – because these people did their duty, with the purest of intentions. And if someone reacts in a negative way to something you have done with the best intention – do not feel hurt, just remain detached. You cannot stop other people from having their own reactions, you cannot go into them – so limit yourself to scrutinizing with all sincerity your own thoughts and intentions. Just listen to this: Gandhiji once injected a calf for a peaceful death. He, a Vaishnava [26], the protagonist of non-violence, the symbol of goodness and a true follower of Indian tradition, a killer of cows! He knew that the Indian masses would be terribly shocked by this worst of moral and religious crimes, and that many would turn their backs on him. But he accepted this, having been convinced that there was no cure for the suffering animal. He did what he felt to be his duty, regardless of good or bad results for himself.

Steadfast wisdom

In Mahatma Gandhi we see a shining proof that the ideal of steadfast wisdom, drawn in the last eighteen shlokas of the second chapter, can be striven for, and attained even by a man who is active in the world. In verse 54, Arjuna asks: "Krishna, what is the description of a man who is firmly established and absorbed in Brahman? How does one of steady wisdom speak? How does he sit? How does he walk?"

To be "absorbed in Brahman" is the definition of samadhi, and therefore, many commentators say that Arjuna is asking for the characteristics of one who is in such a state, united in deep meditation with the transcendental goal of his meditation, and who is coming out of that state. I differ from that view. Arjuna is not interested in such a passing experience; what he wants to know is how he can reach steady wisdom, become firmly established in Brahman, not only with the body sitting motionless, but also when he is active, without fear of falling out of this union again. When you study carefully the following eighteen shlokas, up to the end of the second chapter, you will see this clearly. In a wonderful way, they give guidance on how to attain, not only that fugitive state of samadhi in meditation (dhyana samadhi), but that other, permanent samadhi, in which a man – whether sitting, walking, or talking – just lives in God, always (sahaj samadhi). Such a man has reached that ultimate goal beyond which there is nothing more to strive for. And when his body, this only hurdle on his way to oneness with Brahman, is overcome, he merges happily with Him.

Lord Krishna begins his answer to Arjuna's question (shloka 55) with a principle: Just as one who wants to cultivate a plot of land must first clear it, a seeker must first cast off all desires of the mind. As the plot brings forth only the plant that the cultivator wants to grow, his mind is then free for the Self from which alone contentment can come. Happiness lies only in thoughts, and thoughts never come from the outside. When a person lives without desires, taking happiness from within, then he is a man of steady wisdom.

How can one attain this? Shlokas 56 ff. add some practical advice to the theory, telling us to control our emotions and our senses. Our actions have results. Often we are afraid of these results even before they come: give up this fear! When the results are unfavourable for us, we get angry: control your anger! When they are favourable, do not crave for more and more! Do not be unhappy about adverse results, and do not be overjoyed, dancing like a monkey, when they are favourable.

But why should we not give ourselves to happiness if something has turned out in our favour? Because it is important how you form your nature. If it is affected by good results, it will be affected by bad results also; you will speak evil, and think evil. So always remain unaffected, and do your work steadily! Your joy should never be exuberant, and if sad events come your way, your sorrow should not remain uncontrolled.

It is so simple. Good and bad results are not in our hands. What is in our hands is how we take them. This is the real meaning of shloka 57. So do your duty with all sincerity, work as much as you can, but do not let the results affect you emotionally. Abuse and admiration are in thoughts and words – so control your thoughts and words! Be above liking and disliking – and remain alert to this, even in small things.

Shloka 58 brings an excellent picture: as a tortoise withdraws its head and limbs when danger is near, so man should withdraw his senses. Controlling them in this way does not mean that we should not use them. But we should let in only good things, shutting off all that is evil, all that stirs our worst enemies, the desires. Arjuna, Mind, must bridle the horses, that is the senses. One who achieves this kind of restraint has started off in the right direction. It is not easy, because the senses are very strong, and even if you win a battle against them, it is only a temporary success:

> Even a mind that knows the path
> can be dragged from the path;
> The senses are so unruly.   (60)

So long as man is alive, his mind, his nature is there, whether he be an ordinary man or a saintly person. And so the struggle goes on, and you must be constantly alert. The power of the senses may have become weaker – but at any unexpected moment it is there again. A diseased donkey is too weak to kick, but as soon as it gets better, it will kick the man who has put ointment on its wound: it lies in its nature to kick.

We were travelling, five Swamis, in the Himalayas. One of us picked up a snake that was nearly dead with cold. During the night, in the warmth of a Tibetan house, the snake revived – what excitement! All that is in the snake's nature had returned. . . .

Not thinking evil, not speaking evil, not admiring, not hating, not desiring does to your senses and to your emotions what the cold did to that snake. But it does not kill them. Your effort must be constant, and you must keep watch continually. When someone begins practicing control of the senses, the senses grow very angry. When the mind turns away from them, they lose their food-giver. Vedanta has the following picture: the senses are the ten wives[27] of a man. When he goes away, they weep. Nobody can kill the senses – and we must not try to kill them, because they are God-given, and can be a wonderful help for man, if controlled and used properly.

Even if, under constant control, the objects of the senses cease to exist for a seeker, the taste for them, the attachment, the desire may still be there (59). Mastering the senses is an important step, but it is incomplete as long as desire lives on in the mind. How can one eradicate it? The second part of shloka 59 says that even this taste for objects of the senses will cease once the seeker sees the Supreme.

A new element now comes in. It is the first time in the discourse that "the Supreme" is mentioned. Once you have seen it, all your desires go, as there will be no room for them in your mind any longer. Or the other way round: once all your desires are eradicated, you will see the Supreme. To give up desire, and to search for the Supreme, are two aspects of one and the same procedure. Take this picture: A priceless diamond lies in a small box which, again, is packed in many layers of packing material. When we have taken off the outermost of these layers, we are a little nearer to the diamond; we continue throwing away wrapper after wrapper – till we find the diamond.

This diamond is the Supreme, the Reality – God, Atman, our innermost Self. The wrappings are the desires we must cast off in order to find it.

But where do we obtain the energy for that constant battle against the senses and desires? Immediately after warning Arjuna about the difficulties, Lord Krishna shows the way:

> But he controls the senses
> and recollects the mind
> and fixes it on me.   (61)

When all your wisdom, all your efforts, are not enough to control your senses and to eradicate your desires, when you are defeated after trying again and again, the moment comes when you become aware of human limitations, and you cry out: "O God, help me!" Only when he has been given enough kicks and blows from the senses, from his emotions, from desire, will man search for help from the right authority – from God. So long as you have not experienced this need for help, repeating His name is just an empty, mechanical habit. Only when a rude shock makes you aware of your own helplessness do you realize the greatness of the name of God – whichever of His many names you may use. There is no need to say "Ram Ram" or "Jesus, Jesus" all the time, or to sit motionless in meditation for hours upon end. But we must do it a little bit every day, in the right way, from the bottom of our hearts.

This is the devotion of which shloka 40, Chap. II says that even a little practice can protect one from great fear. It is just as a room is immediately immersed in light if, in the dark, we put our finger on the right spot, where the electric button is.

Indian literature is full of wonderful stories that describe this cry to God in great distress, and the immediate response. I just remind you of the amusing one in the *Mahabharata*, when proud Draupadi, helplessly given over to the enemy who starts pulling off her sari, realizing there is no one to defend her, gives up her pride and cries out to Lord Krishna – who immediately comes to her rescue by giving in more sari around her body than the enemy is pulling off from the outside, till finally, tired and defeated, the villain gives up his evil action.

Whatever you keep thinking of becomes part of you, whether it is good or bad: this is the meaning of shlokas 62 ff. The nearer we get to something by concentrating on it, the more it gets hold over us. Man is free to choose on what he wishes to concentrate: on the external world, or on the centre of the world within, the Atman. If you let the outside world get hold of your mind, there is no end of desire, and when it becomes impossible to satisfy all one's desires, man becomes frustrated, angry, and finally loses life's purpose by the chain of evil that develops from this. But the man who is free from attraction and repulsion, from admiration and hatred, walks safely among the objects of the senses. He achieves peace, real and permanent happiness from within.

But even if what you concentrate upon is good in itself, you must still keep a careful watch on the back door, through which the senses may defeat you: During twelve years of lonely practice in the Himalayas, a Swami has mastered peace. He comes down to the plains, staying in the house of a family. One morning, while he is meditating, a little boy comes into his room and turns on the radio. "Go away!" the Swami shouts. The boy runs, the Swami turns off the radio. But he has no sooner closed his eyes in meditation again than the boy comes back and starts the game over again. The boy laughs, the Swami shouts – and finally he throws the transistor radio, which hits the boy's head. He falls unconscious, and the Swami calls for help and laments: "I have mastered peace for nothing!" He was a great scholar who had studied and practiced – but when anger took hold of him, he forgot all that he had learnt, and destroyed all his understanding and enlightenment.

So be on your guard constantly: the flame of an oil-lamp will move with even a little draught. The mind wavers, not able to take a right decision, when there is external disturbance. But when you listen carefully to the voice within, and hear it clearly, the door will be shut to the draught, the disturbance from outside. Such a controlled, steady mind knows that the Atman is present, and meditation becomes possible, and peace and happiness will be attained. Krishna calls his disciple "mighty-armed". This expression means that Arjuna (i.e. man, and of all creatures, only man) possesses the strength of understanding which will enable him to walk this path of self-control. In shloka 69, "night" and "day" are used as similes: the self-controlled person lives in the light of Reality, and the outside world, in which the ignorant lives, is darkness to him. It is not that he does not take notice of it – but just as the ocean remains not unmoved, but unaffected by the rivers that flow into it, the wise man is never disturbed by the desires that keep flowing into his mind. He is like a man who walks in a rose-garden without being scratched, just inhaling the delightful perfume. So try to be clear-sighted, concentrate on God, avoid attachment to worldly things, then no harm will come to you from them.

To become free from desires and longing, to act without selfishness, egoism and pride: this is the state a person should attain in life – whether it is only just before death, or years earlier, does not matter. Go on trying and trying, so as to get nearer to the goal. Once you have reached it, you will never fall back from it into delusion – and at the moment of death, you will achieve liberation, union with Brahman.

Here ends the second chapter, which has also been called "One-chapter Gita". As we said earlier, it contains the essence of the main teachings of that wonderful book: the knowledge of the nature of man, of his real Self (jnana), and the ways that lead to its realization (yoga). The chapters that follow will lead us deeper into this teaching.

3
Karma-Yoga, or the Path of Action
(Gita III–VI*)*

Arjuna is greatly perturbed by Krishna's words. If the knowledge of Brahman is superior to action – why then does Krishna want to push him into this violence against his own kin? Arjuna now questions him very directly: "Your statements seem to contradict each other. They confuse my mind. Tell me one definite way of reaching the highest good." *(*III, 2*)* In answer to this direct question, Lord Krishna sets out to explain in more detail those paths to perfection and to union with God that an individual may choose, according to his prevailing tendencies. He begins with karma-[28]yoga, because it is the easiest, activity being life itself. Ordinary action is karma; when the love of the heart is applied to it, it becomes yogic activity, karma-yoga. No other yoga can be practiced without the help of karma-yoga: breathing, meditating, reading, singing the name of God – everything is action – action which will lead to perfection only if it is performed with love. There is no such thing as achieving perfection by merely abstaining from action; yogic action is always the first step to any kind of yoga. So first of all, one must know what right action is, and what is meant by freedom from action.

Various steps of action

No work is in itself inferior to any other; everything depends on the intention, the inner attitude, with which it is done. Work is done by the body and its value depends on what a person puts into it. The priest in the temple who, while reciting mechanically from the Vedas, thinks about the money he hopes people will give him for doing so, does work of lesser quality than the sweeper who lovingly sweeps clean every corner of the court-yard, thankful in his heart for having been

36

given such an important task. Both of them will receive their material reward, but we cannot measure by a material rod the happiness the sweeper has in addition. The priest performs his task, the sweeper is on the path of karma-yoga [29].

Two friends go to Hardwar [30], one as a devotee, the other as a tourist. The devotee wants to take a ritual bath in the river, the other is disgusted by the dirt, but does not want to offend his friend by showing it. So they both bathe in the river, the tourist as quickly as possible, overcoming with difficulty his disgust, the devotee praying with great intensity. The water, the physical immersion, is the same. But the other, the spiritual purification, will only benefit the one who has love and devotion for the beliefs connected with the holy Ganga (Ganges). His love purifies his mind, that is, it takes away from him bad thoughts and evil tendencies.

Without purity of mind, no real knowledge, no enlightenment, will be achieved. Once there was a great rishi [31] who had sent his son to school. When the young man returned after twelve years, the father found that his son had studied, but not experienced essential knowledge. He told him that he was to go to yet another master and sent him to a person named Tuladhar ("the balance-holder"). The son expected to see a great sage, but to his surprise he found only a humble shop-keeper. "What am I to tell you, who are such a learned scholar?" Tuladhar said when the young man had explained the purpose of his visit. "The only thing I know is this: I must keep my eyes on the beam of my balance, so as to keep the scales even, the same for all my customers, whether young or old, rich or poor. That is all I can tell you." And the young visitor realized that concentration on the beam of life, on duty, is a prime necessity and the key to everything else.

These are but a few of the innumerable stories that have been told and are still being told, to bring this fundamental truth home to educated and illiterate people alike. Whatever you do, do it to the best of your ability, with love, with devotion, without thinking of reward, for its own sake. Then the obstacles which lie in everybody's path to svadharma – egoism, greed, pride, sloth, desire – will be removed and you will make progress. Let us give just one example that is closer to your own everyday life: Two young men are engaged by an office, on the same day, for the same work, with the same salary. The first interprets duty as slavery; he just works to receive the salary at the end of the month and does as little as possible, without any interest in the work. The second sees the work as his svadharma; he applies his mind to it, he is interested in the activities of the firm. At the end of the year, the first is sacked, the second is promoted, being given not only more money and more responsibility, but also trust, respect and permanent security. Most important of all, he is happy and satisfied with his everyday life, and he develops mentally and spiritually[32].

The karma-yogi puts his whole heart into his activity. Working with such an inner attitude demands less and less effort; it becomes the nature of a karma-yogi. Such work gives joy, and it will seem to him that he is not working at all. He attains freedom.

This kind of action is called vi-karma, which leads to a-karma, to non-action. When you put vi-karma into karma, it becomes a-karma. These terms help us to understand the development of work from toil and drudgery to happiness and joy.

In *Gita* IV, 17 the three steps of action are mentioned, but vi-karma is invariably translated as "forbidden", "unlawful", or "wrong" action. In my opinion, this is an incorrect translation, taken over by one commentator from another. It was Vinoba Bhave who saw this mistake, and if he achieved nothing else but this he would certainly have gained liberation! The prefix vi- has several meanings, but it is quite obvious that here it can only mean something higher, and not something lower than ordinary karma, because the *Gita* always explains things in an evolutionary way, progressing from a lower to a higher level of consciousness[33]. Moreover, as we said in our first chapter, the *Gita* is not concerned with evil action, but with Arjuna, the good man, whose mind is momentarily confused by his attachment for his relatives, overshadowing his devotion to duty. Krishna is leading him to a right understanding, step by step, from karma to vi-karma and to a-karma – naming the steps in IV, 17, and warning his disciple that the real nature of action is difficult to understand. After this, many examples of vi-karma are given. Only when the true nature of action is fully realized, does freedom from action become possible[34]. Vinoba was an excellent linguist and knew Sanskrit perfectly. I think, however, that the difference in interpretation is not due only to the several meanings of a Sanskrit term, but rather to a different approach. Most people think in terms of the opposition between "good" and "evil", and therefore even the great scholars did not notice the error. Vinoba spoke with the confidence of truth, as one who has gone beyond the "pairs of opposites" (see Gita v, 3).

Action and non-action

One who has become aware of the truth, who has found peace in the Atman, has nothing to gain by action, and nothing to lose by refraining from it. But, says the Gita (iii, 20 ff.), the wise man goes on working, with the motive of setting others, by his example, along the path of duty. He knows that people will imitate a great man, and that if he stops working, they, too, will do so. They will sit down and close their eyes, thinking that this is meditation. In this way they will become mere idlers and fakes. Therefore, not wanting to confuse the minds of those who work for the fruit of action, he continues to work, free from egoism, his heart fixed on the Lord: such work is real worship.

All through the fourth chapter, Krishna speaks about the development from karma through vi-karma to a-karma. But Arjuna still cannot grasp this teaching, and he says: "You praise renunciation of action, and then again yoga of action. Now tell me definitely: which of these is better?" (v, 1) This is how the mind (remember that Arjuna is the mind and Krishna is the Atman!) functions: without giving up attachment, he would still prefer to avoid his duty, and therefore he cannot accept what goes against his wishes. And now, Krishna gives an answer which is not easy to understand. Both yoga of action and renunciation of action, he says, lead to the highest bliss – but if you ask me, I would say that yoga of action, or karma-yoga is better.

39

There is no real difference between the sannyasin who renounces physical work and the karma-yogi who renounces the fruit of his work. The karma-yogi does everything, but does not feel that he is doing anything; the sannyasin does not feel that he is doing anything, yet he is doing everything. So the difference is only in the order of the words. Karma-yoga rightly performed and sannyasa rightly performed lead, in the end, to the same goal. But because action lies in our nature, the path of karma-yoga is easier, and therefore better. Moreover, sannyasa also starts from karma. Before you can renounce action, you must act. Nobody is born a renunciate! Action is the root; if karma-yoga is practiced from the very beginning, sannyasa will come as the fruit of maturity. The only way to reach the state of a-karma (karma-sannyasa-yoga) is through karma; everything else is self-deception, as it goes against the laws of nature.

At the beginning of the fourth chapter, Lord Krishna says that He first taught karma-yoga to Vivaswat, the Sun, who in turn taught it to Manu, the first thinking man, who again passed it on to the following generations. Notice the symbolism: the sun is both, an ideal karma-yogi and an ideal Sannyasin. He shines and shines, but thinks nothing of it. That is karma-yoga. He does not think he is working, yet he is giving life to all creation. Even before he appears above the horizon, the birds start chirping, the flowers open . . . the sun makes all living creatures act and work. This is the way of the Sannyasin.

Another example: there was a great sannyasin whose name was Yajnavalkya. King Janaka, a great karma-yogi, was his disciple and he, in turn, taught Suka Dev who became a famous sannyasin. So you see: a karma-yogi learning from a sannyasin, a sannyasin from a karma-yogi: there is no difference!

When the whole active energy of an individual is concentrated fully on one point, his life becomes completely still: this is called a sannyasin's way. In his non-activity, there is the greatest and highest activity. You cannot easily see it, just as children playing with a top think that the top is standing still when it is actually spinning very fast indeed.

Sannyasa looks like stillness, but in reality it is the most intense activity [35].

Let us take a simple illustration: a mother tells her young son: "Don't do that." He goes on doing it, and she warns him: "If you do not listen to me, I shall not talk to you any more." And she remains silent, whatever the boy may do or say. After a while, he will come to her crying: "Oh, please, mother, break this silence – I'll never do it again – beat me, but speak!" In a way, she had done nothing, but the effect of her silence was greater than that of her words.

This example of "acting through silence" reminds me of an incident that happened in ancient Jodhpur. The long, steep hill on which the old Fort now stands was once the place where a great yogi used to stay. When it was decided to build a Fort there, the yogi took a burning brand from the fire and put it into a piece of cloth – so great was this yogi that the fire did not even burn that piece of cloth! – and moved to a small hillock which stands near that great rock. This place soon became a place of pilgrimage, and has remained so to this day. When other yogis, Swamis, naga babas (naked renunciates) travel in the region, they stop on that hillock. Once, some 200 years ago, a Swami came to that place – tall and healthy, wearing only a small loin-cloth, and with a chimta (fire-tongs). Soon it was rumoured that a very holy man had arrived, a complete renunciate, who did not talk at all. From his throne, the Maharaja (who held his durbar – public audience – every day) could see the place of the yogis, and he sent some people to find out about the new arrival – but they could not, because he just remained sitting there in silence, with closed eyes. The Prime Minister tried, in vain, and the Maharaja offered a great reward – without result. Finally the court poet, a clever and witty man, undertook the task. He joined the people sitting around the fire and after a while he asked the man next to him, pointing to the muni baba (silent renunciate): "Do you know him?" "No", came the answer, "nobody does, he never speaks – he is a very holy man." – "It is difficult to say anything about such great souls", said the poet, "but I seem to remember something. Once I went to Hardwar for the Kumbh-mela [36], and when I came out after my ritual bathing in the holy river, I saw people crying over the body of a child who had been drowned. A Swami came along. "Do not cry", he said, "the child is alive". And the little child began to smile, its body moved. When the parents, overwhelmed with joy, finally turned round to show their gratitude to the Swami, he had disappeared. This happened many years ago, and so I am not quite sure – but I think it was this Swami." The silent man nodded in confirmation. "Next time", the poet went on, "I saw him at the Kumbh-mela in Prayag (Allahabad). A milkman had brought his cow to the mela grounds, to serve the pilgrims with milk. One day, the cow's calf died. The cow cried, the milkman's wife cried, the milkman cried . . . and now I am quite sure that it was this Swami who came along and put his chimta on the calf, just as he had done for the child at Hardwar. And the calf, which had been dead for several days, jumped up, full of life – and the Swami walked away. Am I right, Swamiji?" And with open eyes, the baba nodded "yes". "Now, with all certainty, my friends, I can tell you that our third meeting was at the Ujjain Kumbh-mela. There, this very same Swamiji was walking through the market. A sweetmaker was there, very busy with all that big crowd of customers. The Swami quickly took some jalebees (a kind of sweet) from the table, but when the sweet-maker saw him, he ran away, and many people ran after him and he was beaten up."

Now the silent baba jumped up and shouted: "Jhutha, jhutha . . . liar, liar!" "No", said the poet, "you are a jhuta, not I – if I was right twice, why not the third time?"

So you see: so long as there is not maturity and sincerity in action, nobody is enlightened – and when people cease to act, you may take it that they are either highly enlightened or utter fools! Real sannyasins are very rare indeed. Most of those who make credulous people believe that they are holy men, great yogis, great rishis, are nothing but frauds!

Let us consider another aspect of karma-yoga: when we work, we come into contact with many people. That contact brings with it jealousy, love, hatred, admiration, anger, all these emotions. By our reactions we can learn to watch ourselves. When we put our clothes out in the sun, all the khatamals, the vermin, run away. The sun is knowledge – when we come to understand the bad things within ourselves, they run away. So all the people we meet give us the wonderful opportunity of getting to know ourselves. Without contacts, we lack this possibility. We must not seek out evil companions, but if such people come our way, we have to deal with them. How good or how bad others are is no concern of ours – but they all give us the opportunity of getting to know ourselves. If we avoid all contacts, if we always meditate alone among stones and trees – with whom should we quarrel? How can we recognize our own faults and weaknesses? So, mastering peace, attaining real sannyasa, cannot come without our first going through the activities of life.

The key-principle: Control of the mind

I told you that the path of karma-yoga is easy, but when you start on it, do not think the goal is near at hand. Nobody can become a doctor without studying! He must learn his lessons properly and pass his exams; if he is still ignorant, he cannot just come after the required number of years and claim his diploma. The same applies to the karma-yogi: at "primary school", he learns how to work; the "high school" teaches him to concentrate on a subject, thus achieving mastery over it. At the same time he learns to discriminate between important and unimportant actions. Only when he has learnt this can the "University" – if he is gifted – lead him to vi-karma and to a-karma.

A devotee goes on a pilgrimage. Every step that brings him nearer to his goal also brings him happiness. One day he sees the flag on the temple rising from the plain, then the spires and domes of the temple, then the whole temple. And when he finally enters, he stands face to face with the image of his chosen deity. The same applies to the karma-yogi. What is essential is the continual advance in the right direction. This will cleanse his heart from ego, pride, guilty conscience, and every step towards perfection will give him happiness. In the end, bliss and realization will come automatically. Our progress along the path of svadharma is like a pilgrimage.

So long as we have this body of ours, we cannot be one with

our goal – God. The body is a storehouse of weaknesses; perfection is only for the soul within, the Atman. The realization of God is becoming aware of this perfection, and those who know the straight path and walk along it are enlightened. We see the temple – the goal – from a distance; once we are in it, we do not see it any more; we are in God, and our outer existence ceases. The body is a wonderful means, a vehicle for our pilgrimage. Use it for this purpose with all happiness, keep it clean, give it what it needs. But even if you attain realization, you will become thirsty again after you have drunk, hungry after eating, and the senses have to be controlled as long as the body is with you. An athlete has to train his body regularly to become, and to remain, fit. In the same way, constant training in self-control will give you mental strength, and happiness.

Notions like "perfection", "purity" and "realization" are similar to terms of geometry (which is truth). We cannot give a full definition, but we learn by supposition ("suppose a point has no extension – a line has no width"), and come closer and closer to understanding. Even with the fullness of karma-yoga or sannyasa, it is impossible to reach oneness with God as long as we are in this body, but our efforts towards that aim make us truly assured of this fundamental oneness. And when the body, this covering of the Atman, falls, the goal will be attained. This is the meaning of liberation.

In the third and fourth chapters of the *Gita*, Lord Krishna explains karma and vi-karma; in the fifth and at the beginning of the sixth, he speaks in a very poetical and captivating way about the two aspects of a-karma – highest karma-yoga and sannyasa. Arjuna's doubts about his duty now begin to subside; however, he questions the possibility for man to take the path of karma-yoga, and to live in union with his real Self. So, in the sixth chapter, Krishna teaches him the practice of karma-yoga, which, in a word, is discipline: control of the senses, the mind, the body and speech. Such self-discipline gives great strength, and the impossible becomes true. It is here that the greatness of an individual lies.

When Gandhiji set out from Ahmedabad on the salt-march [37], an American journalist asked him: "What is the power by which you dare to challenge the mighty British

44

Government?" "I have no physical power", Gandhiji said, "my strength lies in self-control." – It was this strength that made even the greatest intellectuals follow him like shadows. In the ancient scriptures it is said that Lord Shankara (Shiva) has three eyes. The third one had always been there, but he knew nothing of it, and so he never used it. When the God of passion was about to overpower him, and all he had achieved seemed jeopardized, he concentrated – that is to say, he used self-control – and then the third eye, the eye of knowledge, opened and indiscipline was burnt to ashes. So, when you are self-controlled, all the obstacles on your way to karma-yoga become nothing but dust, and you learn, not how to kill, but how to use your mind and your senses properly, in order to achieve your divine goal.

Full concentration is needed for one who wants to start true meditation. Therefore it is here, in the sixth chapter, that Krishna teaches his disciple the art of dhyana-yoga, or meditation. He mentions such things as seat and posture, but only because they help towards that absolute concentration, that "one-pointedness" of the mind without which no meditation is possible.

Our daily lives give us ample opportunity for practicing self-control. It begins with moderation in everything. Eating just to please the palate, and eating more than your body needs, is bad – but excessive fasting is just as bad. People are drowned because too much water goes inside them – but without water we die. No sleep, and sleeping too much; not speaking, speaking too much . . . these are the things with which self-control begins, and self-control is the first step to karma-yoga. If we keep a diary and give an honest consideration to what we have done during the day, we shall find that a great deal of time has been spent on useless gossip and other unnecessary things, and we shall make an effort to avoid such things.

It is very easy for Europeans to practice karma-yoga; they are quite close to it, because they like to work hard. I have seen even Presidents of European countries doing their own housework! But what many of them lack is love, that spiritual love which knows no egoism, and gives happiness and bliss. Such

45

love cannot easily be taught – but if they do not learn it, they are certainly going to ruin what other generations have built up with great effort all over the world. The Big Powers have undoubtedly created great problems – but if, instead of using their strength for self-interest and war, they would use it for the common good, they could work wonders and make this earth a paradise.

Most Indians, on the other hand, are far from karma-yoga. When Europeans start working, there is no end – and when Indians start talking spirituality, there is no end! Absurd ideas about spirituality and work have developed in India: people think that a religious man should not work with his hands, and yet Krishna, their most beloved God, is the very example of one who works. In the *Mahabharata* we are told that when the others went to rest and evening prayer after the day's battle, Lord Krishna brushed down the horses, put ointment on their wounds and fed them with his own hands. And at a great festival, he took upon himself the task of clearing away the leaf-plates after the meal. Therefore everyone should understand the divine aspect of work. In India, I have in my own small way tried to set an example, together with a group of students, by building roads and cleaning villages. People came in crowds to see a Swami digging the soil and using a broom (oh, those blisters!). Other Swamis said that I was spoiling the people – but later they came to understand my intentions.

It is only by hard and intelligent work that Indians will be able to solve the terrible problems of their country. So both are needed, spirituality and work. And that is why I say to Indians: "Open your eyes and work!" and to Europeans I say: "Close your eyes and meditate!" Self-control is necessary for both.

4
Bhakti-Yoga, or the Path of Devotion
(*Gita* VII–XII)

Having explained karma-yoga, Lord Krishna now speaks of another, a most attractive and essential, means by which man can reach his ultimate goal. He explains in a wonderful way God in His creation, and man's union with Him through bhakti, that is devotion, or divine love. All yogas further our inner progress, but bhakti is the highest, the most important of them all, without which the others cannot succeed. We wash our clothes with water. Soap and all sorts of powders can help in the process – but without water they are of no avail. Bhakti is water among the means for spiritual development.

Four kinds of devotees

Presenting four devotees in different stages of evolution, the great teacher explains how divine love develops from one stage to the next (VII, 16). First comes the devotee in distress; one who is in distress makes an effort to find a solution. That is the second stage. He who seeks will find the way to a solution. That is the third stage. And when he has found the way, he will walk in it. He has reached the fourth stage; he is enlightened and has achieved steadfast wisdom.

The four devotees are all called virtuous, purified by their good deeds, noble and generous. If such people are "in distress", it may be that, like Arjuna, they find themselves in an inner conflict concerning their own true duty, or that they suffer for the miseries of others. They will cry to God for enlightenment, and they will seek for knowledge that may enable them to help sufferers.

Most translations say that they are seeking "wealth". However, noble and generous people, true devotees, never being egoists or materialists, what they are seeking is the wealth of

47

knowledge, the means to help others. One who has found true knowledge is called wise; he will adhere to that knowledge forever, and serve God by serving his fellow-men.

Lord Buddha was such a one. He suffered the pains of the aged, the sick, and the dying, and he left all his luxuries, his wife and son, his palace, in search of something to counteract their suffering. And when at last he found it, he preached unceasingly his gospel of compassion and universal love. Or take Gandhiji: when he came to South-Africa, he started seeking a way out of the sad condition of the Indians there. He found that non-violent resistance was the best way – and this remained his way ever after.

There have been great devotees of this kind in all ages, in East and West. And there have been, and still are, many others who may not be quite so great, but who are nevertheless imbued with this kind of divine love, this urge to serve. You find them in the field of the medical and social services; the history of research is full of examples where people have risked their own health in order to find remedies against suffering. Those who live and work with such love are great devotees. They are the "doers of good deeds", who are freed from delusion and, steadfast in their vows, worship God. *(VII, 28)*

Death is the greatest guru

In the last shlokas of the seventh chapter, Lord Krishna mentions God, Brahman, Atman. Now Arjuna wants to know more about these, and about the nature of this world and that of man: Mind has understood that it is essential for man to know who he is if he wants to find his right path – and Atman answers his questions[38].

It is due to ignorance that people live as they do, addicted to the pleasures and dejected by the miseries of this passing world, doing wrong instead of striving for the realization of the divine within them. And then, when death approaches, they suddenly understand that they have wasted their life. Death will teach the truth to those who have not learnt it in good time. That is why Indian philosophy in general, and the *Gita* in particular, lays emphasis on the need to remember death. This rouses fear, certainly – but fear is a means of reminding man of his duty in life. Christian teaching does the same; so whether we believe in rebirth or not, it is essential to fight an attitude of indifference, of "live, love and be merry", as was taught by materialistic schools of Indian as well as of ancient Greek philosophy, and as is practised so widely in our own day.

A poor man complained to a Swami about a rich man in the village who kept harassing him for a small debt. The Swami went to the rich man, who welcomed him, asking what he could do for him. The Swami took out a needle: "Please take this needle", he said, "keep it with you, and bring it with you when you die, because I shall need it there." "How can I do that?" the rich man asked, "it is impossible". After much argument, the Swami finally said: "If you are not able to take even a needle with you, when you die, how then can you take your great wealth, which you have accumulated in this world by fair means and foul?" The rich man understood the lesson and changed his life.

Just one more of our many stories: Once there was a king-dom, and it had a law that, whosoever came to power, could remain on the throne for only three years. During that time, he was free to do whatever he wanted, but at the end of the third year, he was taken by force to the river, where the people would kick and abuse him, and then send him in a boat to the other shore, where he was left helpless in a forest full of snakes and tigers. All the rulers would spend their three years in merry-making, not caring about the welfare of the country and its people, because they knew of the inevitable end. But once there came a monarch who, taking the simplest room in the palace to live in, started working hard from the first day, asking his Minister of Finance to inform him about the state of the treasury and acquaint him with the needs of every village, and then he saw to it that everybody was given food, water, education and medical facilities. In the second year he had the jungle on the other side of the river cleared, and when the third year started, he sent young people there to construct irrigation works, cultivate the land and build houses.

At the end of the third year, the king walked to the river and asked the boatman to take him to the other side. All the people came and implored him not to go, but he insisted that this was the law of the land. So finally the boatmen took him across – and when he arrived, instead of tigers there were the young people to welcome and to garland him, and they led him to a royal house. . . . The three years symbolize the three stages of life; the King had wasted none of them.

Man leaves this world either on the path of light, the path of no return, or the path of night, which will eventually take him back to human birth, says the *Gita* (VIII, 23–28). The whole explanation sounds most mysterious, as if man could choose the time of his death. You must take this as an allegory: In the first half of the year, the sun is on the northern path; it is the period of light. After its turn to the southern path, monsoon clouds pile up over India, and after the rainy season the nights get longer and the smoke of hearth fires hangs over the villages. It is the period of darkness. The time of the waxing moon is the bright fortnight; the moon wanes in the dark fortnight. The meaning of all this is: Do not die in the clouds of ignorance! Do not waste your life in the darkness of idleness but use your days to free your mind from the smoke of attachment, by the flame of devoted action, in order to open your heart to the clear light of knowledge. If you live in this way, you will be in a state of enlightenment at your last moment – you will know how to die. It is your life that decides whether you depart weeping or smiling.

The royal road

The *Gita* is like the Ganges: it is holy everywhere, but just as there are, on the banks of the river, some places of pilgrimage where people come in their millions, so, in the *Gita*, there are some chapters of particular importance. These are the chapters II, IX, XII, XV, and for some people also XVIII; many rishis have left their mortal body reciting one of these. The ninth chapter is the heart of the six chapters on devotion – it shows the royal road, the road of complete surrender to God. Its principal shlokas are 11, 14, 15 and 26–34. Shloka 11 says: "Fools pass blindly by the place of my dwelling, here in the human form, and of my majesty they know nothing at all, who am the Lord, their soul."

Most people search for God somewhere far away, in an unknown and distant place, and do not understand that He is of much easier access in what is very close and well-known to them: in man – in oneself and in others. How great is this ignorance! First, man must realize God in man, because that is where He is nearest; thereafter, man will be able to see Him everywhere, in everything, and in all the deities that are nothing but His countless aspects. Whatever a bhakta (devotee) will give and do to others, he will give and do as an offering to Him – and God will accept everything that is given and done in true devotion (shloka 26 ff).

"Even those born of a sinful womb, women, traders and labourers can attain the highest realization, if they take refuge in me", Lord Krishna says in IX, 32. This testifies to the darkness of those times when it was thought that only the male members of high castes, intellectuals, warriors and rulers, could attain liberation. They alone were allowed to read the holy scriptures and to perform the ritual of the divine sacrifices. It was into this ignoble society that God Himself was born:

When goodness grows weak,
when evil increases,
I make myself a body.
In every age I come back
to deliver the holy
to destroy the sin of the sinner,
to establish righteousness.

(IV, 7 and 8) [39]

Lord Krishna came as a revolutionary, to put truth back on the throne of truth. Even to-day, society is very low, because those who are strong want to monopolize the good things of this world; but the Gita makes it quite clear that in the eyes of God, your family, your birth, your sex and your profession are of no importance at all. What counts is the purity of your mind, the true love in your devotion.

The royal road is wide and straight, so that everybody can walk on it even with closed eyes. But some courage is needed for the start. You must make a final, a definite decision. Just as no marriage is possible without a firm decision, the decision to surrender to God cannot be valid for one day and not for the next. Do not think that your nature is too bad, forget your weaknesses, your bad habits and all the evil acts you may have committed in the past – just jump into this Ganges of devotion with all your faults, and your heart will become pure. We surrender with all that is good and all that is bad in us, with our body and our senses, and therefore, abiding by our decision can change our nature and our life. Once our eyes have become God's eyes – how can they see anything bad? How can we speak evil when our tongue has become His tongue? How can we hear evil with His ears? If somebody speaks evil of others, they will not listen. When every part of the body, brain, senses, mind and intellect have become God's, there will be nothing but waves of divine thought within you. The change in your nature will not come suddenly, it needs practice. But if you bear your decision firmly in mind, there will be no room for evil thoughts, and nothing bad can pass your lips. Gradually, all your activities, all your thinking, become acts of worship. Those who are able to surrender in this way, will have that direct, intuitive knowledge mentioned in IX, 2; bhakti is for them the easiest means by which to achieve the highest goal – the realization of the Divine in the Self.

One in All

Arjuna now fully accepts the divine teaching, having understood meanwhile that, through the familiar form of his trusted friend and charioteer, God is speaking to him. His heart goes out to Him; he asks Krishna to name all the shapes and powers under which He may be known. (X, 17 and 18)

And once more we observe the divine teacher going deeper into a question about which he had already spoken, making it easier for his disciple to grasp the full meaning of the fact that God supports everything – that He, the One, is in all. Krishna names the highest of deities, of humans, of abstract notions and of qualities, as being identical with him. But if he says, for instance, "I am Himalaya among the things that cannot be moved", "I am the strength of the strong", or "I am Arjuna among the Pandavas", etc., it does not mean that God is not in smaller mountains, or in the other Pandavas, or even in the weakness of the weak – but it is easier for the mind to visualize Him in what is mighty and admirable. Yet after a long and impressive enumeration, Krishna adds: "But what need have you, Arjuna, to know this vast variety? Know only that I exist, and that one atom of myself sustains the Universe." *(x, 42)* This is indeed the one thing that man needs to know.

In the Vedas, another mode of easy approach is shown. It begins with what comes first in everybody's life: "See God in your mother." A mother gives birth – God is the beginning of everything. The mother provides what the child needs – God does the same for all creatures. A mother always thinks good of her child – so does God. A particular mother may have her faults – but the ideal mother is a symbol of an experience beyond any physical form. If you close your eyes and meditate on this, you will experience this flowing river of all pure love. And look at the sweet face of a little child! There is no cunning, no selfishness . . . and this is why people worship God in the infant Jesus, and in the little boy Krishna.

You should see God in your father, then in your teacher. Your guru imparts knowledge – he wants nothing more than to give and to help, expounding the truth to the disciple who sits with him. I dislike the expression of "sitting at the feet of the guru". They just sit together – and if, one day, the guru's understanding is surpassed by that of his disciple, the guru will be as happy as a father to whom a child is born! How could he possibly accept any fee for his loving effort? So-called gurus who take a fee, or who exploit the ignorance and blind faith of the innocent people who come to them with their problems, are either fakes, or very, very selfish. Sincerity, honesty, no trace of any selfish desire, love for someone who is not a son, not a daughter – these are among the essential qualities of a guru. Once the disciple understands this, he will be ready to serve the guru, to do all he can for him, of his own free will. This physical body is not the guru – it is merely a vehicle for this experience, the guru's love for the disciple who opens the door of his heart to knowledge and enlightenment. Words cannot express this relationship of pure and selfless love. This is God in the guru – and in this sense it is correct when people say that the guru is God.

You may experience God not only in human beings but also in animals, in inanimate things even, if you transcend their physical boundary. Let me give you a few examples: Mother Earth gives and gives – and though we tread on her, she continues to give. And the clouds give rain, withholding nothing. Water is something physical, but when you sit on the shore, you can experience that power behind the roaring waves of the sea, the grandeur behind the continued flow of the Ganga. The scent of a beautiful rose – breathe it in deeply, and you experience joy and peace. The beauty of nature is outward, but it can rouse in you the feeling that God is everywhere. Close your eyes, reach out – you can reach out by the sound, by the odour, by the colour – and when you reach that boundary beyond which there is nothing but love and devotion, then adhere to it with the innocence of a child. Such meditation can be very, very helpful for feeling, deep within ourselves, the ever-active presence of God [40].

All in One

He who has realized that God can be experienced in everything, will see Him when he looks up, when he looks down, to the left or to the right. Arjuna has grasped this "One in All", but the enquiring mind is not satisfied, seeking yet another way: he wants to see the "All in One"; he asks for a vision of God in His universal form.

Psychologically, the request is understandable, but as a material experience it is impossible. All things that are in this "All" change, come and go; the "One" remains, unborn, undying.

Man has a tendency to accept the existence of only what he can see with his own eyes; when he is given "divine sight", that is to say, wisdom and understanding, he will realize, and experience what is beyond the visible. This is what Krishna grants to Arjuna, the excellent man and devotee. We come to understand that four things are necessary for such an extraordinary experience: An individual

1. who, by his good acts in former lives, has been born with intelligence and a devotional inclination,
2. who, in this life also, has sought God sincerely and honestly,
3. who has enjoyed the guidance of a qualified person, and
4. who has obtained God's grace.

Of these four things, only one is in human hands – and that is the second, one's own efforts. We have no power over our past Karmas[28], nor can we count on finding the right guru. Moreover, we have no right to the gift of God's grace. But if our efforts are honest, we should not worry about the third and the fourth conditions. They will come of themselves. "When a disciple is ready, the Master will come" goes the saying. This is even more true for the grace of God – when the time is ready, it comes even if we fail to pray for it.

For Arjuna, all the four conditions were fulfilled, and so his wish was granted. In a grandiose description, we are told how Arjuna beheld "the entire universe, in all its multitudinous diversity, lodged as one being within the body of the God of gods". *(XI, 13)*

Arjuna was overwhelmed by the sight; "his hair stood on end", *(XI, 14)*, and finally he cries out: "Tell me who you are . . . have mercy: I desire to know you." *(XI, 31)* And Krishna reveals himself as "the mighty world-destroying Time, now engaged in destroying the worlds. Even without you, none of the warriors arrayed in hostile armies shall live." *(XI, 32)* And he admonishes Arjuna to do his duty, to conquer the enemies, seeming to slay them who have already been slain by the great Destroyer Himself: "Be thou a mere instrument, oh Arjuna." This is the most important thing here, not the order to slay as such, but to become an instrument of God's will.

The intensity of the revelation becomes unbearable to Arjuna. So long as he is in this physical body, man cannot see God permanently. Only when the separate identity ends, when Atman becomes Brahman, does the drop become ocean – man merges into God. So Arjuna prays Krishna to show his

55

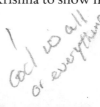

familiar human form again. Krishna consents, and consoles his bewildered devotee. *(XI, 45–50)*

Let me repeat: The easiest and most noble way is to see God in man. To serve man is to serve God. This is the Kingdom of Heaven for those who become an instrument, who can hear and obey His commands. Just as a bamboo flute that has nothing of itself left within it, can produce sweet sounds . . . This eleventh chapter is very dear to me.

Name and form: the right beginning

Arjuna has fully understood the essence of bhakti, and he now asks a very spiritual question: "Which way of devotion is better – to worship God in the manifest or in the unmanifest?" *(XII, 1)* This question has given rise to very learned and very complicated commentaries, but I shall try to explain to you the short yet important twelfth chapter in my own simple way.

Some people worship God as the unmanifest and changeless, seeking oneness with the Absolute, the impersonal Divine. Others seek unity with a personal God, manifest in the world of man, in nature. Which is better? This is what Arjuna wants to know, and Krishna answers that both will achieve the same goal, but from the point of view of practice, worship of a personal God, manifest in the world of man, is better. People who quarrel about the "right" God, or His "right" aspect for devotion, remind me of two blind men in front of an elephant: one holds a leg, the other an ear, and both keep insisting: "This is the elephant!" Such behaviour leads nowhere; we must seek the whole truth.

"Saguna bhakti" is the form of worship which makes use of a name and a form, and therefore appeals to the mind and the senses. Devotees praise Him under one of His many names, or they worship a form, such as a statue. From my point of view, it is not correct to speak of an "idol" – the image is a visible symbol to meditate upon, just as "Ram" and "Om" are sound symbols. Spiritually highly developed people need not make use of such aids; they worship the Absolute without name and form. This is nirguna bhakti. God accepts both. For Him there is no difference between the two. The whole twelfth chapter is a wonderfully clear enumeration of all that makes an ideal bhakta, very dear to God whether he practices nirguna or saguna.

But it is very difficult to realize what is not manifest. Therefore Krishna says that the practice of saguna is the better yoga. It would be sheer folly to begin with nirguna, because the unprepared novice would get helplessly entangled in such abstract thoughts. On the other hand, it would be just as foolish to remain content with saguna for ever; saguna is a means that may be discarded once a bhakta can do without it, just as we discard an empty tin. This worship through name and form has a very scientific, psychological basis. But when it comes into the hands of ignorant people it is completely ruined.

A great Saint advised an unhappy man to pray and worship. "I do not believe in these images", the man said. He had no parents, no wife, nobody to love, only one sheep. "Then sit in front of your sheep and think that it is God", the Saint said. When he came back six months later, he found a completely changed man, reciting the name of God and worshipping his sheep. So you see, man needs a symbol through which he can love God. There is love in our heart, but only when it can flow out does man realize that it is love.

The whole world is nothing but name and form. Life, the Divine within us, has no name, no form – but for understanding we need a form to see, and a name for it. Look at these gold ornaments – a bangle, a ring. When we melt them, the gold is still there, but we do not call it ring or bangle, because there is no form of a ring or bangle any more. If we take the gold away, however, neither ring nor bangle can exist. Take away the clay of a toy elephant – neither form nor name will remain. In man-made things, both name and form are given by man; man also gives a name to things made by God. This world is name and form, but it exists only because of that great truth – God.

This is how the worship of name and form must be understood. Hindus have been very severely criticised for it, but in reality there is no religion in the world that can do entirely without name and form. Once again, let us take the example of geometry, that mother of science: The teacher draws a line from A to B, saying: "This line has no width." A student gets up and remarks: "But Sir, we can all see the width!" Immediately, the teacher corrects himself, saying: "Suppose it has no width!" This "suppose" is said with the aim of teaching something higher. Even reading and writing is possible only because we have learnt to accept that the letter A "is" a certain sound. In reality, sound is shapeless; the whole alphabet is nothing but accepted supposition and, without showing its form, it cannot be taught. If the pupil has no faith in the word of the teacher that this sign "is" A, he can never learn to read and write, never experience the joy and sorrow, never grasp the high thoughts and ideas contained in the pages of a book.

The same holds good for devotion. "Suppose the sound Om is God" – "suppose this piece of stone is Krishna." When this statue was carved in Jaipur, nobody worshipped it, nor when it was packed, shipped, unloaded and unpacked here, and left lying about for months. When then did it start to "be" Krishna? When there was a ritual to fix this "suppose" in it. But if you stop there with the supposition, without going deeper down, you miss the gold of truth, the real content of the message that the statue carries.

Before the great festival of Durga puja in Bengal (and also in other Indian States), people make beautiful clay images of the Divine Mother, in accordance with their own imagination. During the puja they sing, dance, weep, worship and hear lectures before the image, and when it is over, they immerse that image in the Hooghly, or the Bay of Bengal – and that is the end of them. Their purpose has been served.

So these images render great service when used properly – as a means, as a beginning. Real worship starts from name and form, whether from images, man, or nature. But it does not stop at these ever-changing things. Do not think you have reached the goal before you are able to worship the nameless and the formless, the changeless and the eternal – standing face to face with that great power which has no name, no form.

5

Jnana-Yoga, or the Path of Knowledge
(*Gita* XIII–XV)

13

Arjuna eagerly wishes to know more about that great power which has no name, no form, and its relation to man. This knowledge, or right discrimination between the mortal body and the immortal soul, Brahman-Atman, is indeed the most important knowledge that man can acquire, and chapters XIII–XV explain, as far as words can explain, Brahman and Prakriti (nature), and man's relationship to each of these. This supreme knowledge is the "jnana" of the *Gita*, which cannot be grasped by the intellect alone but must be grasped also by intuition and experience; it is vi-jnana[33], and it pervades our heart, our entire being. Jnana-yoga is the basis of that wisdom which leads to right action. We have said before that each individual will give preference to one of the yogas corresponding to his nature, but none of them – karma, bhakti or jnana – can exist without the other two. They are like ice-cream – you may like it for its coolness, its flavour, or its sweetness – but the three blend harmoniously, and you can only eat them all together!

The relation between man and God

The thirteenth chapter explains this knowledge very subtly, starting from a simile. The human body is called the "field", Atman its "knower". Through his thoughts, man sows good and bad seed – his actions, of which he reaps the fruit. The "knower" of the field is also its owner, who watches the changes that take place in it.

Once Lord Buddha came to a farmer's house with his begging bowl. "You seem a healthy man", the tired farmer remarked, "are you not ashamed to beg? Why do you not work on the land as I do, growing your own crops?" "I am a farmer, indeed", the visitor replied, "this body is my field, and I am growing non-violence, forgiveness, compassion, universal love and truth". He who understands will sow the best seed and reap the best harvest of this transitory life. That is to say, he will develop all the virtues within himself.

An ignorant person is like a playing child who is not aware that his mother is watching him; he does not feel that God is an omni-present "witness". When he grows in understanding, he feels the voice within, which says, "very good – very bad" to whatever he thinks, says or does. It is the "supporter" that speaks, as shloka 22 calls the Atman. If you watch people, you will see the awareness of this showing on their faces.

When man has come to understand that, without the help of God, nothing can be achieved, and that when he prays for it sincerely, the "fulfiller" rushes to him, a close and permanent relationship is established between mortal man and the immortal God within him. One who can discriminate between the two is called a jnani, a man of knowledge or enlightenment. He will know how to work in the field, leaving the fulfilment to the divine energy, and by so doing, he achieves life's purpose: the realization of the Divine within himself and in the universe[41].

Do not take this to be merely abstract, theoretical knowledge; it is the foundation on which our karma builds a house in which to live a life beautified by bhakti and governed by jnana, free from the fears of this transitory world. In XIII, 7–11, the *Gita* names the qualities of a jnani. Study them, and you will see that they contain much more than what we usually subsume under the term "knowledge". All that goes against these good qualities, their opposites, is called ignorance (Shloka 11).

The nature of man

This knowledge, right discrimination, is not easy: again and again, man succumbs to the illusion that his real Self is his mind, his intelligence, all that makes his phenomenal ego. Therefore, in the fourteenth chapter, we are led to a deeper understanding of the nature of man.

The creative power of Brahman is the basis of all mind and

matter. This power is called prakriti, or maya, both terms really meaning the same[42]. Brahman, the Absolute, is beyond action. When we think of Him united with his acting power, we call Him Ishvara, who creates, preserves, and destroys the universe. He is then regarded as a personal God, as God with attributes, and is given many names. In the *Gita*, Krishna sometimes speaks as a personal God, sometimes as the Absolute. When we think of God in man, we also use different expressions: Atman, purusha, jiva, kutashtha. . . . You find them all in the *Gita*, but you must not be confused by these many names. They denote the various aspects of the Divine, but there is no difference in essence.

Prakriti and purusha, the body and its "indweller", are always together, "they dance together". Nothing can be thought, felt, done, preserved or destroyed unless there is a physical body – nature – and a soul – God within. Nature is made up of three gunas, translated by "attributes", "modes", "qualities", "tendencies", "principles", or "constituent factors". One translator has also spoken of "the three strands forming the rope of Maya", binding man to the manifest world. Each of the gunas is contained, to a different degree, in all things in nature; they also express themselves in the temperament, in the mind of man, in ever-changing combinations. Supplementing the lower tendencies by the higher ones means to develop our character.

Tamas is characterized by darkness, sluggishness, stupor, inertia, laziness,
rajas stands for passion, motion, activity,
sattva for light, purity, harmony.

We must never permit tamas, which binds us by delusion and ignorance, to hold sway over us. By cultivating rajas, by being active, we can overcome tamas. But rajas will bind us to action, useless action; it will fill us with hunger for pleasure and cause a never-ending chain of desires. So we must not let rajas rule our lives but must use it in a controlled way. The means of control is the cultivation of sattva, the principle of harmony, to which we must give predominance in life.

Sattva must be developed – but be careful! Sattva can bind

us to the happiness it gives, and every binding force is an obstacle on our way. Sattva can fill our ego with pride for being so good, so generous. Therefore continued, ego-less endeavour is necessary to root out ego even from sattva. This is achieved by work performed as worship. When we are able to do this, we progress along our path; we transcend the gunas, which are of the physical world, and we prepare for that perfection which can be fully achieved only once this physical body is left behind.

In the great epic *Ramayana* we find a vivid illustration of the gunas. The *Ramayana*, like the *Mahabharata*, contains a treasure of spiritual truths clad in stories and pictures that even children can understand.

There were three brothers, Ravana, Kumbhakarna and Vibhishana, born of the same father and the same mother. Ravana, the demon-king of Lanka, symbolizing rajas, was the eldest of the brothers. He had enormous powers and all the riches of the world. He had also performed great deeds and was a devotee of Lord Shiva. But he considered himself to be the only devotee, the greatest king. Deep in his heart he knew that he could not equal Rama, and it was out of jealousy that he abducted Rama's wife, Sita. Ravana is pictured with ten heads, symbolizing his insatiability. Ravana was killed by Rama: rajas must be eliminated; God in us must destroy this ego, this passion, this conceit.

Kumbhakarna, the symbol of tamas, was enormous, like a mountain. He slept and slept, and when at last he stopped his snoring, which was like a great gale, it was only because the smell of good food drifted into his nostrils. He then stuffed herds of buffaloes and sheep into his mouth, described as a fearful cavern, and he drank liquor by the barrel. After that he boasted that he would drain the ocean, crush the sun and the moon between his teeth, vanquish the God of death, and Indra, King of "skyland"!

Kumbhakarna also died at the hands of Rama: there can be no compromise with sluggishness, greed and boasting. This is how we have to deal with whatever tamasic tendencies we may harbour in our character!

The youngest of the brothers was Vibhishana. He was all

sattwa, goodness incarnate. When he saw that he could not draw Ravana away from the wrong path, he finally left him and went over to Rama, who in the end made him king of Lanka. This means that we cannot achieve permanent goodness, freedom from fear, steadfast wisdom, before we have surrendered to God.

In each of us, as in the entire universe, there exist sattwic, rajasic and tamasic tendencies. But God has also given us the capacity to discriminate, and the power to clear the bush. Watch the gunas in your character, eradicate tamas, control rajas, and when sattwa predominates, beware of pride and ego. This knowledge is very precious.

Completeness of knowledge

It is extremely difficult to coin words which can express the Supreme, from which come both the perishable and the imperishable within the perishable. The small, soul-elevating fifteenth chapter makes a new and wonderful effort to undertake this task.

It begins with the metaphor of a particular tree, which is usually explained very mysteriously as a symbol for the phenomenal world rooted in Brahman. As I see it, it can also be understood in a much simpler, more direct way. In contrast to other trees, the Indian fig- or banyan-tree grows roots from the branches, down into the ground, supporting the branches, from which they come. I see this as a symbol of man. Whatever we think, say, or do, comes from the brain; the roots of all our actions are in the head, above. The brain is a product of the gunas, just as the branches from which the peepul-roots issue. The body is the trunk, the leaves symbolize all our knowledge, the buds the sense-objects. The name of the tree is asvattha, which means "not enduring till to-morrow"; this mortal creature cannot be perceived here in its eternal reality, nor in its origin and its end. Only when the roots have been cut with the axe of non-attachment can the goal be sought – the eternal Brahman. Think this over, and the symbolic contents of the picture will further your understanding.

Shloka 16 ff.: Two things are in this world, matter and life, the perishable and the imperishable. Together they constitute the world we see around us. Mirabai, the great poetess and royal devotee of the Lord, sings: "My hansa, my swan, my indweller is still young, but this temple, this body, has grown old." Both of them, the perishable and the imperishable, are born of the same source, the supreme Self, God. Neither life nor matter can exist without Him. Let us take this picture: In the light of the sun, we see a pot containing water which reflects the sun. If the sun disappears, we can see neither the pot of water nor the reflection of the sun. The pot is matter, the reflection is life, and both are there only because of the sun above. In the same way, everything in this world, the perishable and the imperishable, exists through the supreme Self. This supreme Self is beyond words, even beyond our capacity of understanding – but we feel that it "is".

Let me give you another picture: There is a master; he has a servant, and the servant has at his disposal some means of performing his tasks. The master is the supreme Self, the servant is the "indweller", the individual Self, and the means is the mortal body with all its talents and qualities and all that it comes into contact with. The servant must make the best use of the means at his disposal, and if he is not there, they are of no use – useless eyes, useless ears, a useless brain. This individual Self works through the body, for the supreme Self that permeates the whole universe, and of which he is, in reality, just a part, a spark. As long as the spark is there, the means must be utilized in a divine way. "One who knows this becomes truly wise: he knows everything that is necessary." (xv, 20) He who understands the relationship between the perishable, the imperishable and the Supreme, will live accordingly. He will always be aware of the existence of the Supreme, of the presence of the imperishable, and he will accept the perishable as a temporary means to be used with the best intentions. So long as the body is there, perfection is only in the purity of the intentions; he, however, knows that his real Self is the imperishable within, and not that which is imperfect and perishable. Therein lies the completeness of life, and the completeness of knowledge.

6

More Advice
(Gita XVI and XVII)

The 15th chapter has shown us the climax of jnana, and there the *Gita* really ends. However, anyone who has understood the teaching and resolved to follow it needs some additional guidance. A new life dawns for the seeker, and chapters XVI and XVII help him to see more clearly the connection between ethics, faith, and God-realization.

Good and evil – the conflict between divine and demonic tendencies

The conflict between good and evil in the human heart goes on from generation to generation. It is symbolized in ancient stories and religious traditions everywhere in the world, and in all of them evil is overcome by good. Lord Buddha vanquishes the demon Mara, Jesus Christ is victorious over Satan, Allah over Iblis, Ahuramazda over Ahriman. In the *Ramayana*, the forces of the demon-king Ravana, though numerically much stronger, are destroyed by the divine forces of Rama. In the *Bhagavatam*, Krishna kills Kamsa, and in the *Mahabharata*, the Kauravas are, in the end, defeated by the Pandavas.

The 16th chapter describes vividly the divine and the demonic tendencies in man. In reality, both of them are to be found in each of us, and this chapter helps us to recognize them, and to develop the good ones at the cost of the bad ones. There is no reason to feel depressed because we see so many bad things in ourselves, but we must not cease our efforts to uproot them.

Three evils are named as being particularly dangerous: "Hell has three doors: desire, anger and greed". (XVI, 21) Self-control, control of the senses, will inflict on these three a crushing defeat. Yet someone who masters self-control and has developed his inner strength often obtains great influence over others. This is where the devil catches even such good men. They so easily fall into the trap and misuse their power, dominating and exploiting others, or developing love of luxury and wealth, becoming proud of their own achievements. Many become conceited of their own religion, their own culture, considering them to be the only true ones. Let us all be vigilant against such evils. Humility will be our guard.

Living in harmony

At the end of the 16th chapter, Krishna advises Arjuna to let the scriptures be his guide as to what to do, and what to abstain from doing. This gives rise to a new question: "There are men who sacrifice to God with faith in their heart, although they do not follow the instructions of the scriptures. What is the nature of that faith? Is it sattva, rajas or tamas?" (XVII, 1) Krishna now explains that the faith of each individual corresponds to his nature.

In order to understand the meaning of "sacrifice", let us revert to Gita III, 10 ff. There, it is said that God created man together with yagna, sacrifice (other editions say "duty"), and from the beginning, gave him all he needs for his living. God gives, man sacrifices. This yagna, this sacrifice, is a kind of give-and-take. Man, like all living beings, is nourished by nature – expressed in the Gita by the "devas", the cosmic powers, but if we do not give back something (for instance organic manure to the soil), it will soon be unable to sustain us any longer. Even the rainfall is affected by man's activity. If forests are exploited greedily, without replanting new trees for those that have been felled, the climate becomes dry, and the soil will become eroded.

From time immemorial, man has experienced the fact that nature cannot be endlessly exploited, and by throwing some food into the fire in yagna, according to Vedic rites, the feeling is expressed that "this is not mine, it is God's." To-day, we have the scientific knowledge and the means to obey this rule of "give and take", but you all know that the preservation of natural resources has nevertheless become one of our biggest problems.

This relationship between man and nature is explained in the third chapter and taken up again in the seventeenth. Those inspired by sattva do not want anything in return for their yagna; they feel they are merely repaying something they have received earlier. The same applies to man's relationship to society. The "dan" which XVII 7, mentions together with yagna, should be translated simply by "giving selflessly", not by "alms-giving", or "charity". Because, before we can speak of "alms", we should pay back to society what it has given to us, ever since we were born[43]. If we understand this, we will refrain from amassing wealth at the cost of others, and if we help those who are less fortunate than we are, we shall do so without that degrading attitude inherent in "alms-giving" and "charity", because we know that we are merely repaying a debt. When we give in this way, we shall never expect any-thing in return – and yet, we shall experience great happiness and feel that we are progressing along our spiritual path. This does not apply only to the material aid we may be giving, but also when we help physically (nursing, for instance), mentally (teaching) and spiritually (leading someone in the right direc-tion). So let us be generous in all these fields.

Together with yagna and dan, *Gita* mentions tapas, aus-terities (physical, mental and verbal). Man must have control over his body, his mind, and his tongue, and tapas is a means of acquiring the strength for this, causing difficulty at first, but yielding great results if we persevere. In India, it is quite common to do tapas, for instance, to remain silent for one day a week, or a month, in order to practice restraint of the tongue, so as never to utter anything that may hurt others. Regular fasting is undertaken not only because it is good for health, but for spiritual development. The time of fasting should be devoted to some divine or good cause, and the food we renounce must go to those who have none. Rich people can give away food even without fasting – but the idea is that they must also experience the pangs of hunger, so as better to understand the wretchedness of the poor, and be induced to undertake something for their benefit. In this way, disinterested service through yagna, dan, and tapas, and spiritual growth become one; the individual lives in harmony with nature, with society and with his own innermost Self.

After having understood that behind the variety of temperaments and outward appearances, all human beings and the entire creation are really one, the highest step has become possible for the individual – to become one with God. Here, the Divine teacher gives his disciple a mantra[44], the mantra Om tat sat. Om is the Absolute Brahman, tat means "that", the indefinable, and sat means highest Reality, highest Being. This mantra has been called the triple designation of Brahman. All acts of sacrifice, study of sacred scriptures, spiritual discipline or meditation begin with "Om" or with "Om tat sat". With this mantra of dedication, we direct our faith and will towards Brahman; uttering or thinking it, we should dedicate all our actions to the Lord, wishing that, day after day, they may become progressively more unselfish, till in the end our own good, the good of others and the supreme good are all one.

7

Summing Up
(Gita XVIII*)*

As bees put honey into the beehive, drop by drop, so Lord
Krishna has given knowledge to Arjuna all through these
seventeen chapters. When, in the end, the honey is taken out of
the hive, we see and taste it in its fulness. Similarly, the
Eighteenth chapter imparts in its fulness that knowledge
which leads to right living, to perfection, and to the attainment
of the goal of life. Though this last teaching may now sound
quite easy, it would not be possible to understand it without
the basis laid down in the foregoing chapters.

Arjuna asks one last question: "I want to learn the truth
about renunciation and non-attachment. What is the difference between these two principles?" *(*XVIII, 1*)*

The question as to which way of life is better for attaining
liberation, that of renouncing the world or that of being active
in the world, was much discussed in the days when the *Gita*
was written. Lord Krishna mentions the various philosophic
opinions and gives his own judgment: to be free from egoism
and from attachment, and with this attitude to be active in the
world, is the advice he gives to his disciple. He explains this in
detail.

Renunciation means the complete giving up of all actions
which are motivated by desires, and non-attachment means
abandonment of the fruits of action. So long as man is alive, he
cannot give up actions altogether. In the first place, he should
renounce all those that are bad in themselves, and do what is
good. Acts of service should never be given up, because they
are a means of purification for those who understand them
rightly, that is, who perform them without expecting any
benefit for themselves. Even then, such actions – as all actions
– inevitably contain a certain measure of evil. Man can be

perfect only in his intentions[45]. The intention that stands behind an act is the touchstone of its quality. A man who can distinguish between desire and renunciation, can also distinguish between right and wrong actions. He who has uprooted all desires knows how to do his duty, whether it be agreeable or disagreeable. And above all, he knows that if he offers all his actions to God, he will not do wrong, but walk securely on the path to perfection.

Such is the gist of the spiritual knowledge which Krishna has bestowed upon his disciple. But he does not want to force it on him: "I have taught you that wisdom which is the secret of secrets. Ponder it carefully. Then act as you think best," he tells him (63). Now that he has fully understood, Arjuna, the mind, is to decide freely how to act and end his dilemma – by giving in to his feelings of attachment, or by doing his duty, by acting on the advice of Krishna, the Atman, the voice of the Divine within.

All through the *Gita*, Arjuna has been asking, asking eagerly, and Krishna has answered patiently. Now, for the first and only time, the roles are reversed: the teacher asks, and the disciple answers:

"Have you listened carefully, Arjuna, to everything I have told you? Have I dispelled the delusions of your ignorance?" (72)

And Arjuna answers:

"By your grace, O Lord, my delusions have been destroyed. I have gained knowledge[46]. My mind stands firm, its doubts are ended. I will act according to your word." (73)

These are the words of one who, from conviction, has taken a free and final decision. The teaching has gone to his heart of hearts. Arjuna's fear is ended, and Mind knows that if he listens to Krishna, the Atman, and acts accordingly, he will be safe. From now on, the two will walk on as one.

Notes and Glossary

1. *Swami:* Master, Lord, also husband. Every Hindu monk who has taken the vow of complete renunciation of worldly desires and duties is called a Swami; here, it is a monastic title prefixed to a monastic name. The majority of Hindu monks wear ochre-coloured robes.

2. *Guru:* Teacher in all fields of learning, but mainly in the religious, spiritual and intellectual spheres.

3. *Yoga:* The term is cognate with the English "yoke" and means "harnessing" or "applying oneself to". In religious practice, it embraces various paths leading to the goal of life – union with God. One who has this goal constantly in mind is leading a yogic life.

4. *Rishikesh:* A place of pilgrimage on the upper reaches of the Ganges.

5. *Sannyasa:* Renunciation of worldly goods and duties. A person having taken the vow of sannyasa is a Sannyasin; sannyasa is irrevocable. It is both the state of institutionalized monachism as well as the last of the four successive phases of the Hindu's life according to pre-Buddhistic tradition, the first three being celibate studenthood, life as a householder, recluse. See our fourth chapter "Action and non-action".

6. *Shankaracharya:* A very famous scholar and sage who lived at the turn of the 8th century. The name was Shankara, the addition "acharya" indicating that he was a very learned commentator and teacher. He founded an order of monks and developed a new philosophy.

7. *Vedanta:* lit. "end of the Vedas" or "climax of knowledge" (root "vid" = to know). The Vedas are the oldest testimonies of Indian philosophical thought, each of them having four divisions. The last of these is called "Division of knowledge", and this is discussed in the Upanishads. This part of the Upanishads is also called "Vedanta". The philosophy of Vedanta affirms the existence of a single impersonal spiritual principle, the supreme conscious Brahman. There are several schools of Vedanta, the main one being that of Advaita, i.e. "not-two", in other words, radical Monism (see also Note 18). The *Gita* is one of the most popular expressions of this philosophy.

8. The suffix *-ji* after a name or a title indicates respect: Gandhiji, Swamiji.

9. For Indians, culture and religion are one. Swami Krishnanand avoids the word *religion* when talking of Hinduism (a word in any way coined in Europe), the word being liable to misunderstanding in this connection.

10. An allusion to the great epic poem *Ramayana*.

11. *Satsang:* "Divine Association", "Assembly of God"; term for any function where communal worship takes place, mostly in the form of devotional songs and prayers.

12. *Deen Bandhu Samaj:* "Friends of the Poor Society".

13. *Casteism:* For "caste" see Note 22. What is meant here are the social evils which have developed out of something that, originally, was basically good.

14. *Vinobaji:* Vinoba Bhave, a saintly man, often called "the spiritual heir of Mahatma Gandhi".

CHAPTER I

15. Age of the *Gita*: For the sake of our more historically minded readers, we may add that, according to generally accepted scientific findings, the origins of the *Gita* go back to the 5th or 4th century BC.

16. Cit. from Glasenapp, "Die Philosophie der Inder", Stuttgart 1949, p. 6.

17. The other two pillars are the Upanishads and the Brahma-sutras.

18. The Sanskrit word *Atman* is translated sometimes by "soul", sometimes by "the (real) Self". Neither expression is fully satisfactory: if we say "soul", we must keep in mind that this is right only in the sense of the soul as "the principle of life in all creatures". All the other attributes which we currently subsume under "soul" (principle of thought and action; seat of emotions, feelings, sentiments, of the subconscious, etc., in short, the "psyche" of the psychiatrists) belong, in Indian thinking, to the world of (invisible) matter. The Atman however, our innermost individual being, is the same as Brahman, the cosmic being of nature and of all phenomena: "As Atman in the body, so Brahman in the Universe." Atman is never affected by our thoughts and deeds. This has also to be borne in mind when using the term "Self" (with a capital S), because although Christian mystics, like the Indian ones, have experienced this complete unity of "God" and "soul" (or of Brahman and Atman), and although we, too, speak of the "divine spark" within us, we in the West are used to thinking of them as distinct and separate: on the one hand man, with all that constitutes him, on the other God as a separate entity – this is the usual pattern of our thinking; it is a philosophy of "dvaita", not "advaita" (see Note 7). In the *Gita*, however, it is precisely this separation between man and the Divine, and our usual identification of the mortal ego, or "self", with our innermost being which is called "ignorance". As for Krishna, who symbolizes the Atman in the narrative of the *Gita*, he was probably originally a historical person, later considered an "avatar" (incarnation) of the god Vishnu.

CHAPTER 2

19. This interpretation cannot be found, to my knowledge, in any other commentary. It was curiosity that made Arjuna drive closer to the army of the enemy; without this curiosity, he would never have seen the familiar faces, and his problem would not have arisen.

20. *Buddhi*, the "interpreter" of our text, is usually translated by "intellect". On another occasion Swamiji spoke of "perception", which he likened to a "judge", or to a "pair of scales", a "thermometer", something giving objective, correct, neutral judgment, or measure. By some authors, "buddhi" is also defined as the power of, or the organ for, discernment between right and wrong. "Manas" is the power of, or the organ for, thinking, usually translated by "mind".

21. That which transmigrates from one body to the next contains all the impressions and deeds of our former lives, which are the basis for the new body, the new life (karma; see also Note 28). It is sometimes called "the individual soul", in contrast to "the cosmic soul", with which it becomes one when the goal of liberation from the wheel of rebirth is reached, as a bubble on the water becomes one with the ocean (see also Note 18). The *Gita* explains karma and transmigration beautifully *(*II, 11–30, and IV, 1–9*)*. Swami Krishnanand does not burden his listeners unduly with these notions, holding that the *Gita* can be understood without them.

22. Some readers may feel that it is preposterous to think of killing as a God-given duty. Here we must remember that, from very early times, every Indian belonged to one of the four orders of society, each of which had its particular tasks. Originally, the choice was made according to an individual's nature (svadharma), and instances of change from one order to another can be found both in the *Ramayana* and in the *Mahabharata*. But in time, choice was replaced by birth: the development of the rigid caste system with its ignoble attitudes and practices had started. It cripples Indian society even to-day, although the country is striving hard to overcome this disgraceful tradition.

As for Arjuna, he never questions his duty as a member of the warrior caste as such; not from the obligation to kill does he shrink back, but from killing his relatives and teachers. Suppose Arjuna were an army leader of to-day, in any nation: could he run away from his responsibilities at the last moment, because he suddenly feels that killing is bad in itself? No – it would be his duty to fight. We should therefore not stumble over the many examples where the *Gita* mentions caste-duty, thinking that this does not concern us, either as Westerners or as modern Indians. Even without castes, svadharma remains: we have our duties in society, and they are merely one among many other factors forming the framework within which our spiritual development can take place (see also Note 29, and our fourth chapter, "The royal road").

23. Krishna uses the word *Sankhya*. We must not understand this to mean the system of Indian philosophy of the same name (main author: Ishvarakrishna), but as the profound knowledge of the Self. Similarly, "Yoga", as used in the *Gita*, has nothing to do with the "Yoga sutra" by Patanjali. We may say that in the *Gita*, "Sankhya" stands for "theory", and "yoga" for "practice".

24. For explanation of the *gunas*, see our fifth chapter, "The nature of man".

25. *Prasad:* Tranquillity, peace, happiness. This is symbolically represented by the distribution, after every religious ceremony, of food that has been blessed by having been offered to God first. Calling this custom "prasad" signifies that divine peace and happiness have come as a result of complete concentration and contemplation during the ceremony.

26. *Vaishnava:* A devotee of Vishnu. The Vaishnavites esteem very highly, in particular, the principle of love for all creatures.

27. Senses: The simile mentions ten wives because, according to the Indian way of thinking there are, corresponding to the five "outer" senses, the five "inner" senses. In other words: the ten "indriyas" comprise five capabilities of "sensing" and five of "acting".

CHAPTER 3

28. "The word *karma* is derived from the Sanskrit kri, to do: all action is karma. Technically, this word also means the effects of action. In connection with metaphysics, it sometimes means the effects of which our past actions were the causes. But in karma-yoga we have simply to do with the word karma as meaning work." (Vivekananda, at the beginning of his "Karma-yoga". Advaita Ashrama, Calcutta, 14th ed. 1970). See also Note 21.

29. The priest belongs to the highest, that is, the Brahmin caste; the sweeper to the lowest, or labourer caste. This makes it clear, as do several other examples given in this book, that the spiritual evolution of an individual has nothing to do with his caste or his position in life (see also Note 22).

30. Hardwar is a very old and holy place of pilgrimage on the upper reaches of the Ganges, where the river issues from a gorge at the southern foot of the Sivalik mountain range.

31. *Rishi:* A seer, a prophet.

32. A particular form of action, sacrifice, very important in the teaching of the *Gita*, is treated in III, 10–15. Swamiji will explain sacrifice, in our sixth chapter, as an integral part of right living. "Living in harmony".

33. We may mention just one other example where *vi-* gives a special, a higher, signification to a word: "jnana" is ordinary, or scientific, knowledge, "vi-jnana" is higher knowledge, the intuitive knowledge of Brahman.

34. In III, 36 Arjuna asks what it is that makes a man do wrong even against his own will, as if under some compulsion. Sri Krishna explains that this is done under the influence of anger and desire. Attachment being a form of desire, man must overcome this elusive enemy by controlling the mind and by spiritual discrimination. Desires and emotions being hard to overcome, Krishna answers this question patiently, although he had already spoken about it before, in a most impressive way *(II, 62 and 63)*. Here, in the fourth chapter, however, where Krishna is explaining the nature of karma-yoga and of renunciation of action, there can be no question of evil action.

35. "A real *sannyasi*, one who is in constant samadhi, and free from all distorting passion – if we keep one such with us for ten days, what light, what energy he radiates! What could not be achieved by repeated efforts through the years, becomes easy because we look at him, because he is with us." This quotation from *"Talks on the Gita"* by Vinoba (Benares 1970, p. 56) may help us to understand the nature of "activity in non-action".

36. *Mela* means fair; the Kumbh-mela is an ancient festival of particular holiness, held at intervals of three years, at Hardwar, Allahabad, Ujjain and Nasik in turn.

37. The "salt march" is the most famous and most inspiring episode in Gandhi's civil disobedience campaign. He started on the 10th of March, 1930 from his Sabarmati Ashram (then called Satyagraha Ashram = civil disobedience retreat) in Ahmedabad, with 85 chosen and tried co-workers on foot, 12 miles a day for 24 days, to a small village on the seashore, called Dandi, to break the law of the British Government and make salt from sea-water.

CHAPTER 4

38. See also our second chapter, "The three basic principles".

39. The incarnation of God in a human body is one of the age-old mysteries. According to Indian belief, however, and in contrast to Christian teaching, this has not happened once only, and must not necessarily be seen in a historical context.

40. The teaching that we have tried to explain in this chapter has often led people to interpret the Hindu religion as merely "pantheistic". Yet if you look at it closely, this reproach is unjustified. Brahman, although it manifests itself in the world, is not confined to it, but transcends it; *Gita* VII, 12 and IX, 4 explain this very clearly. Here is an illustrative picture for what IX, 4 wishes to express: "As waves take their origin from the sea and sport on it, so all beings, from the creator, Brahma, down to the whole creation, even to a blade of grass, take their origin in Brahman (the Supreme) and rest in Him. As the whole sea is not contained in the waves, the Supreme, the unmanifest Brahman, is not contained in the manifest beings. He is infinite while these (beings) are all finite." (Unfortunately, I have not been able to trace the origin of this excellent image.)

CHAPTER 5

41. See also our second chapter, "The three basic principles".

42. The frequent translation of *maya* merely as "illusion" is inaccurate. In the *Gita*, maya mostly means the creative force of Brahman, which becomes manifest in nature, as "name and form"; see also the description of the gunas later in this chapter. The relation of Brahman to maya is described by the analogy of the relation between fire and heat.

In other contexts "maya" means the totality of phenomenal experience and of relative existence as opposed to eternal Brahman, the Absolute.

CHAPTER 6

43. This is why the duty to serve one's parents, as also ancestor-worship, are deep-rooted in many societies.

44. *Mantra:* A sacred and mystical syllable or formula, imparted to the disciple by his guru, for meditation.

CHAPTER 7

45. See also our second chapter, "The right attitude".

46. lit. "memory", meaning "consciousness of my real nature".